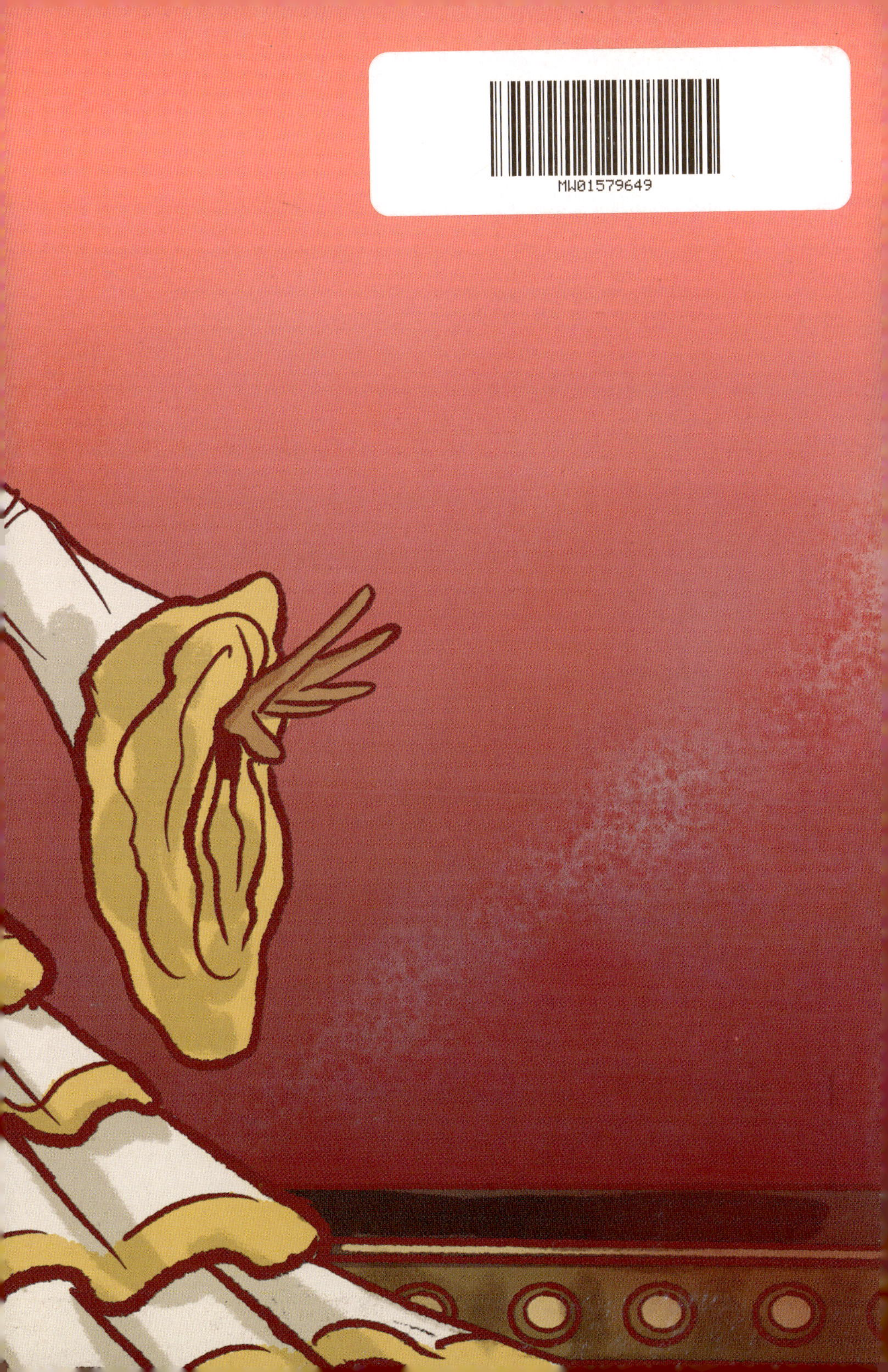

© 2022 Sunbird Books, an imprint of Phoenix International Publications, Inc.
8501 West Higgins Road   34 Seymour Street   Heimhuder Straße 81
Chicago, Illinois 60631   London W1H 7JE   20148 Hamburg

www.sunbirdkidsbooks.com

All rights reserved. No part of this publication may be reproduced or transmitted in any form or by any means, electronic or mechanical, including photocopying, recording, or any information or storage retrieval system, without prior written permission from the publisher. Permission is never granted for commercial purposes.

This book is sold subject to the condition that it shall not, by way of trade or otherwise, be lent, resold, hired out, or otherwise circulated without the publisher's prior consent in any form or binding or cover other than that in which it is published and without similar condition being imposed on the subsequent purchaser.

Sunbird Books and the colophon are registered trademarks of Phoenix International Publications, Inc.

Library of Congress Control Number: 2021952657

ISBN: 978-1-5037-6491-0 Printed in China

IT'S HER STORY

JOSEPHINE BAKER

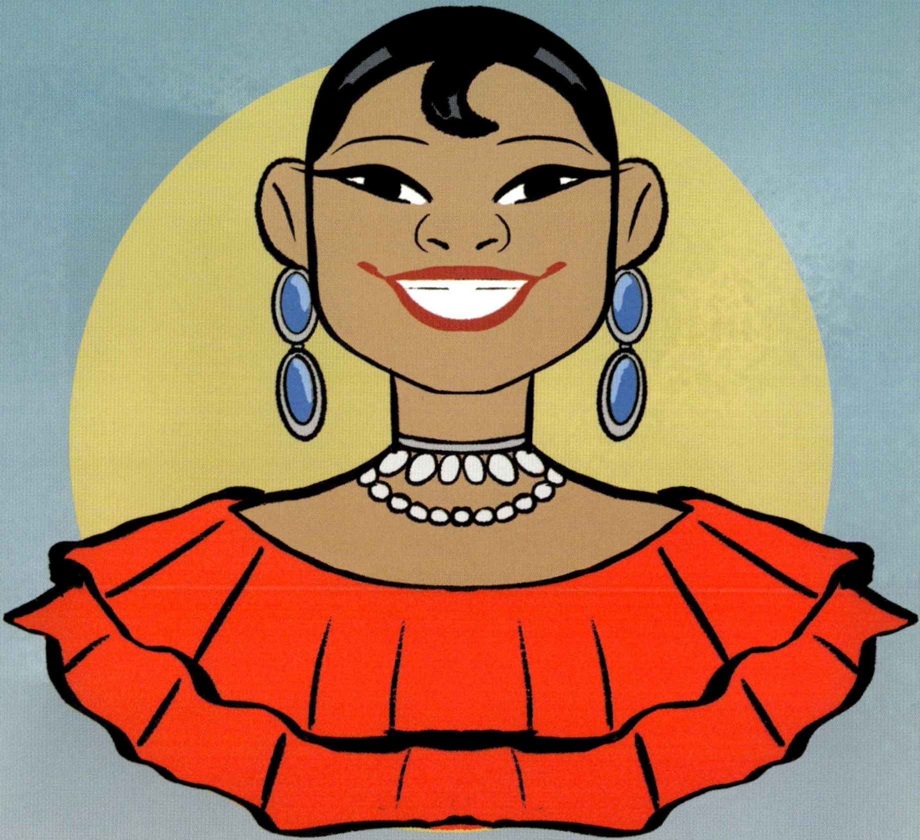

Written by Lauren Gamble
Illustrated by Markia Jenai

sunbird books

JOSEPHINE BAKER

was a symbol of the Jazz Age in Paris, France. She danced her way into people's hearts and became a legend in her time.

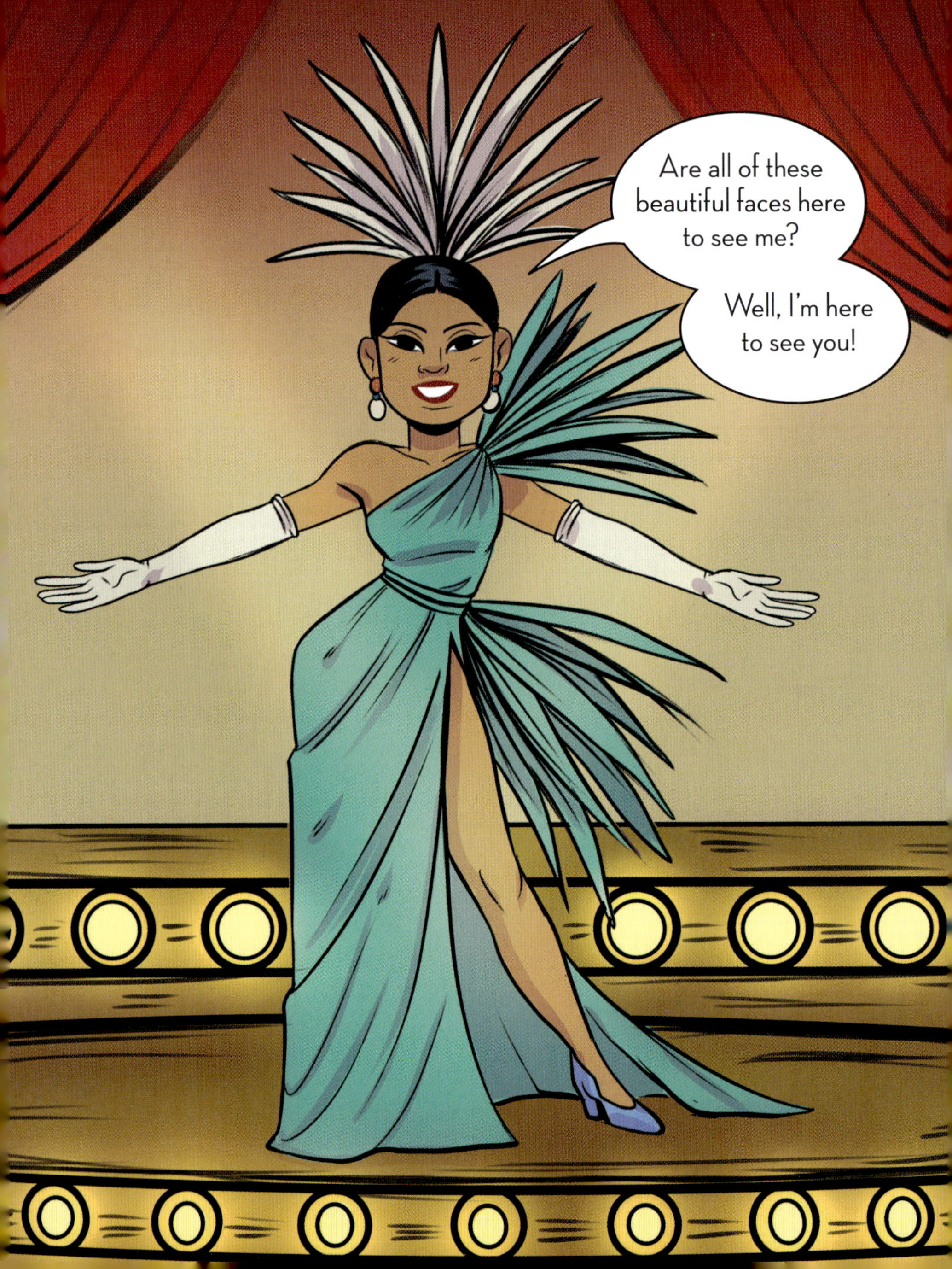
Are all of these beautiful faces here to see me?
Well, I'm here to see you!

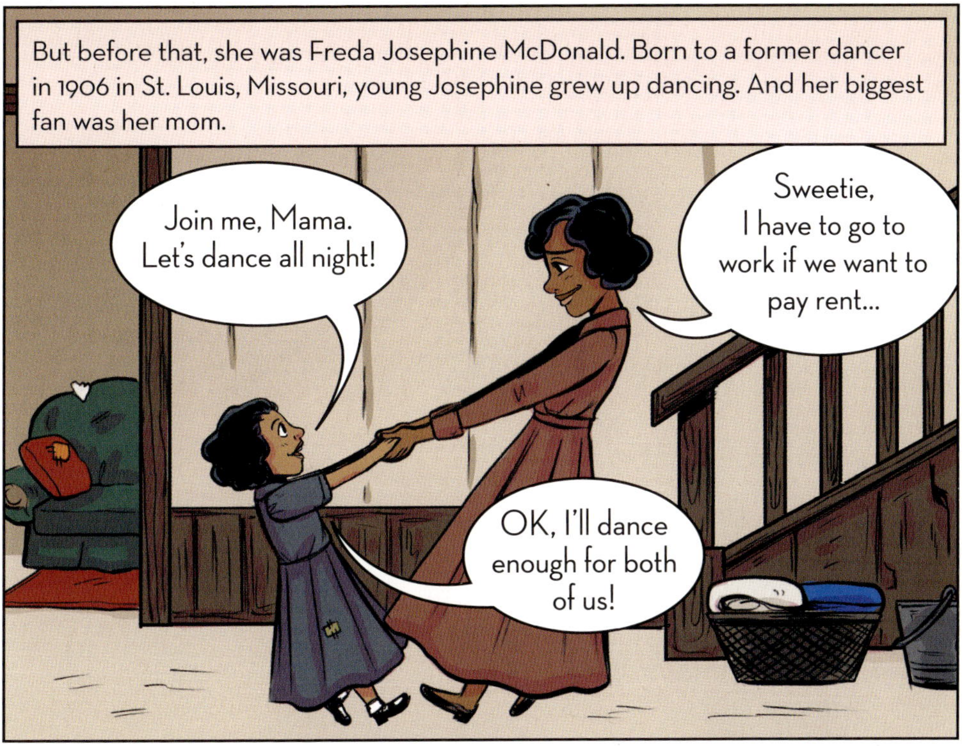
But before that, she was Freda Josephine McDonald. Born to a former dancer in 1906 in St. Louis, Missouri, young Josephine grew up dancing. And her biggest fan was her mom.
Join me, Mama. Let's dance all night!
Sweetie, I have to go to work if we want to pay rent...
OK, I'll dance enough for both of us!

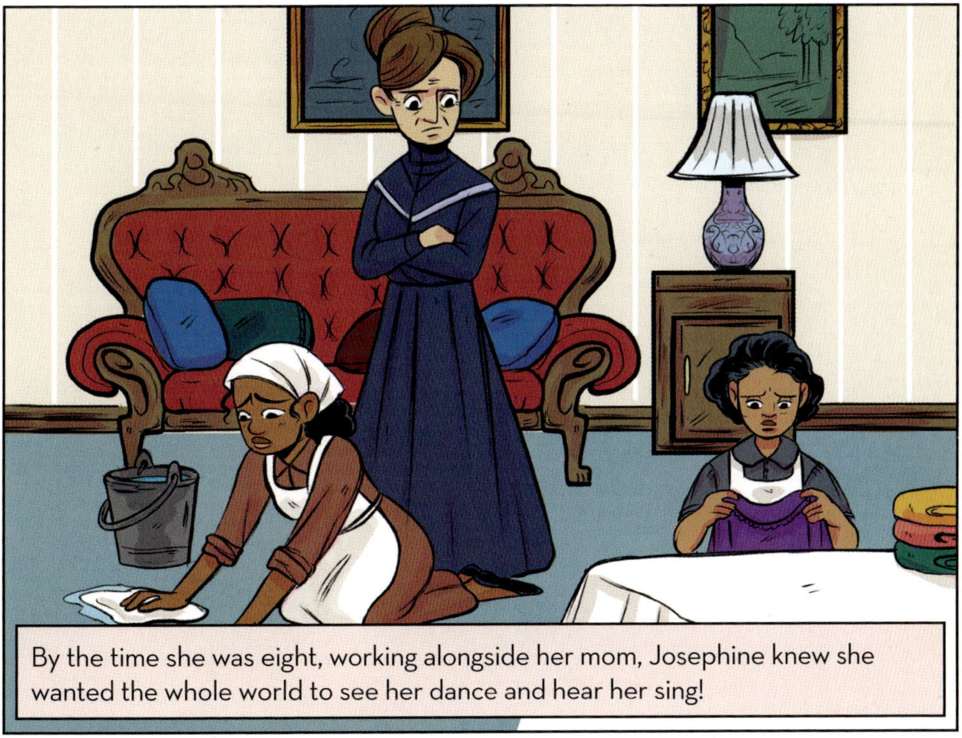
By the time she was eight, working alongside her mom, Josephine knew she wanted the whole world to see her dance and hear her sing!

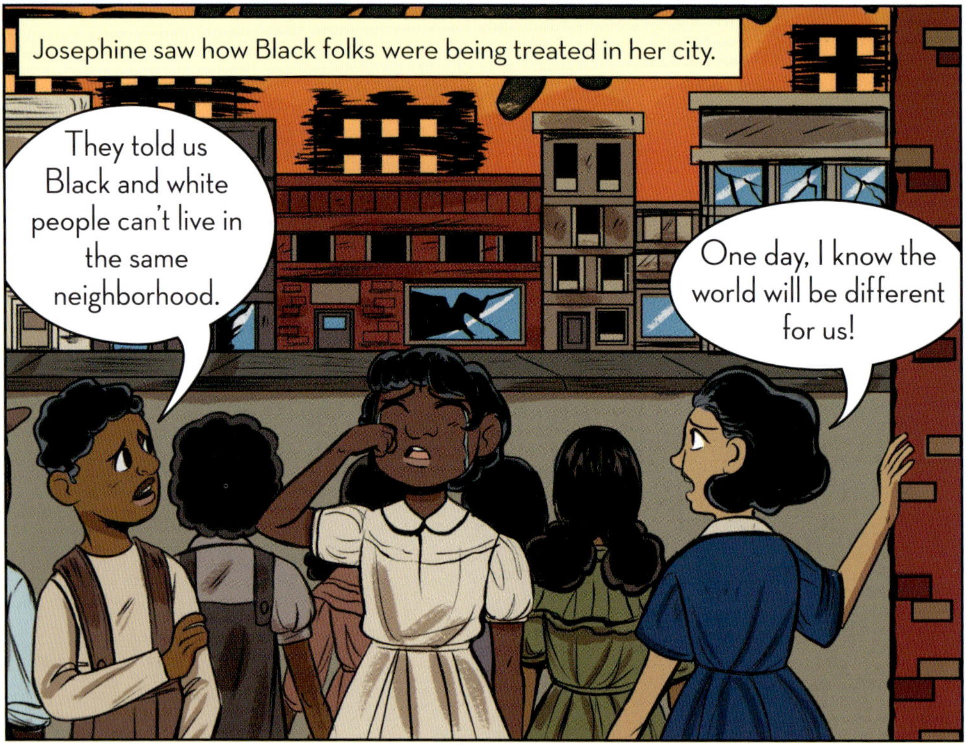
Josephine saw how Black folks were being treated in her city.
They told us Black and white people can't live in the same neighborhood.
One day, I know the world will be different for us!

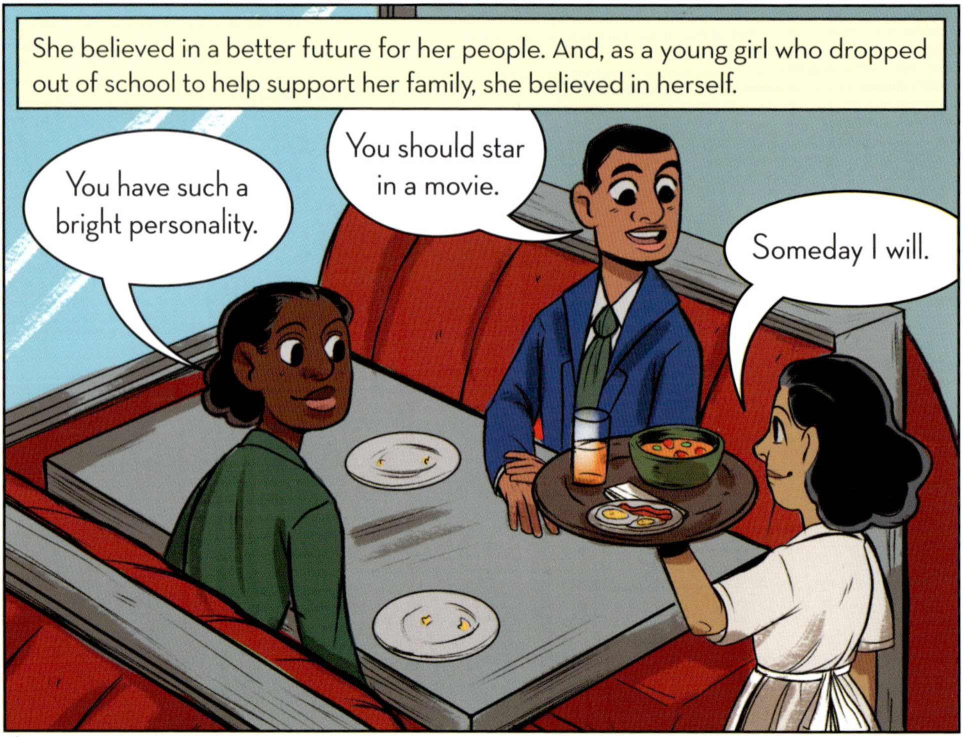
She believed in a better future for her people. And, as a young girl who dropped out of school to help support her family, she believed in herself.
You have such a bright personality.
You should star in a movie.
Someday I will.

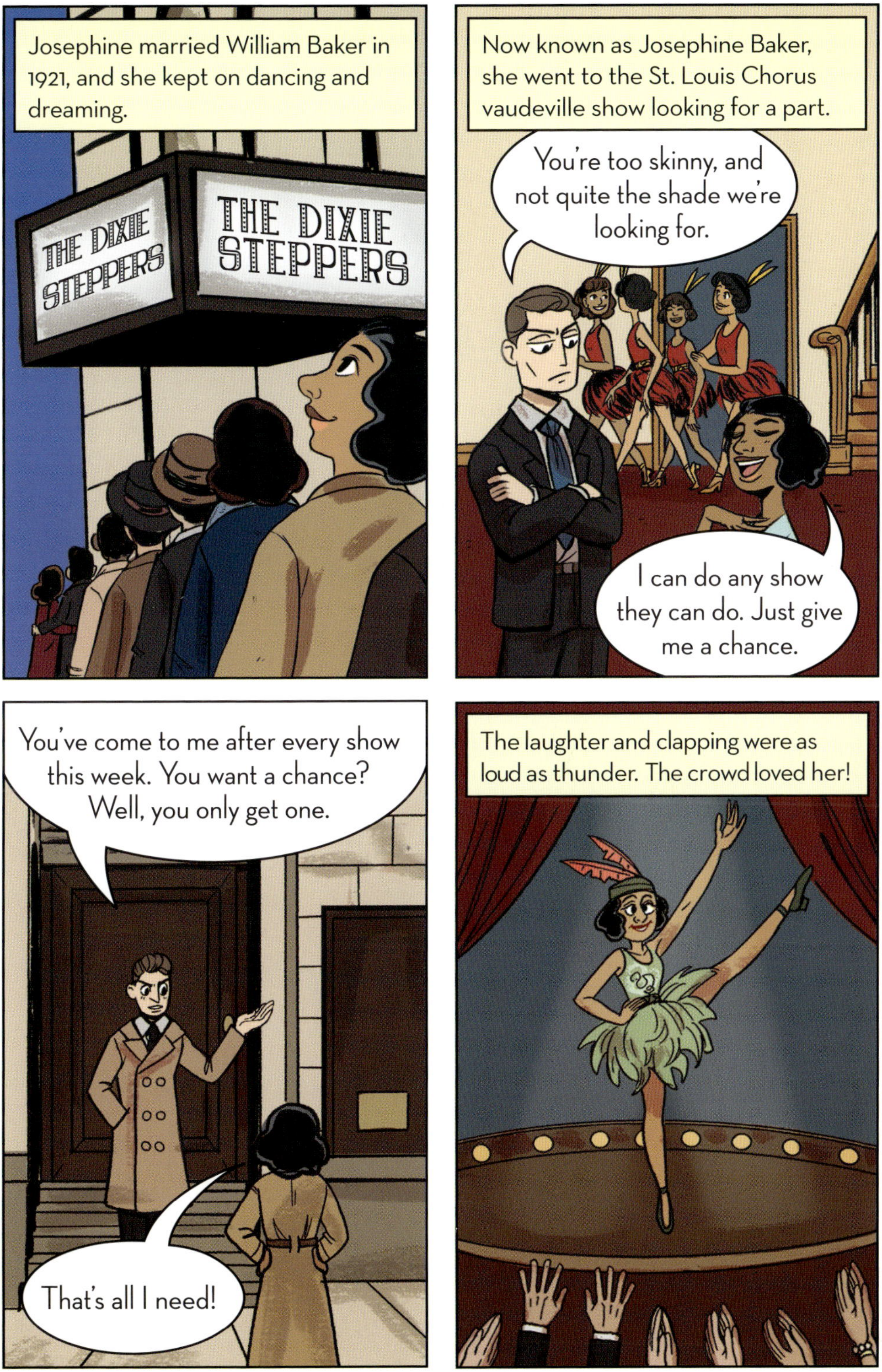
Josephine married William Baker in 1921, and she kept on dancing and dreaming.
THE DIXIE STEPPERS
THE DIXIE STEPPERS
Now known as Josephine Baker, she went to the St. Louis Chorus vaudeville show looking for a part.
You're too skinny, and not quite the shade we're looking for.
I can do any show they can do. Just give me a chance.
You've come to me after every show this week. You want a chance? Well, you only get one.
That's all I need!
The laughter and clapping were as loud as thunder. The crowd loved her!

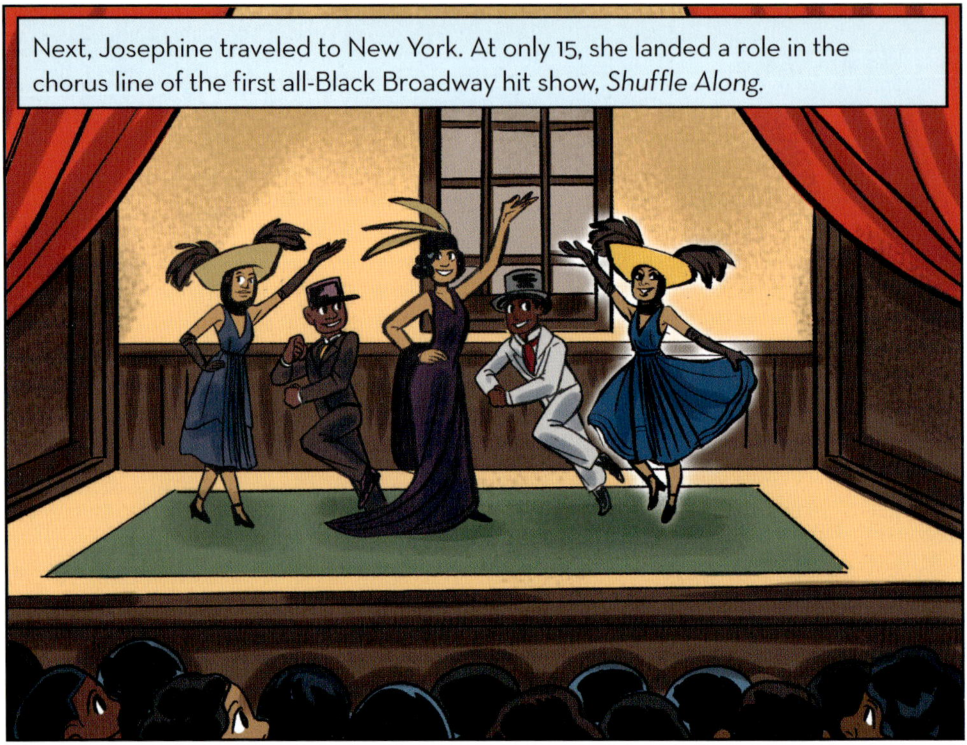
Next, Josephine traveled to New York. At only 15, she landed a role in the chorus line of the first all-Black Broadway hit show, *Shuffle Along*.

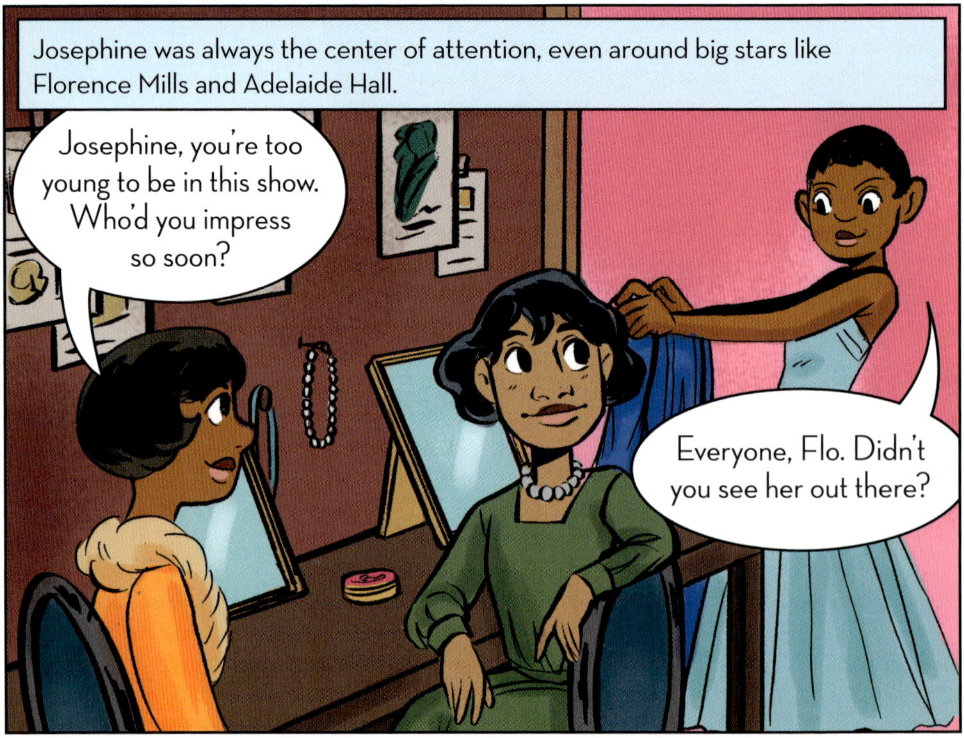
Josephine was always the center of attention, even around big stars like Florence Mills and Adelaide Hall.
Josephine, you're too young to be in this show. Who'd you impress so soon?
Everyone, Flo. Didn't you see her out there?

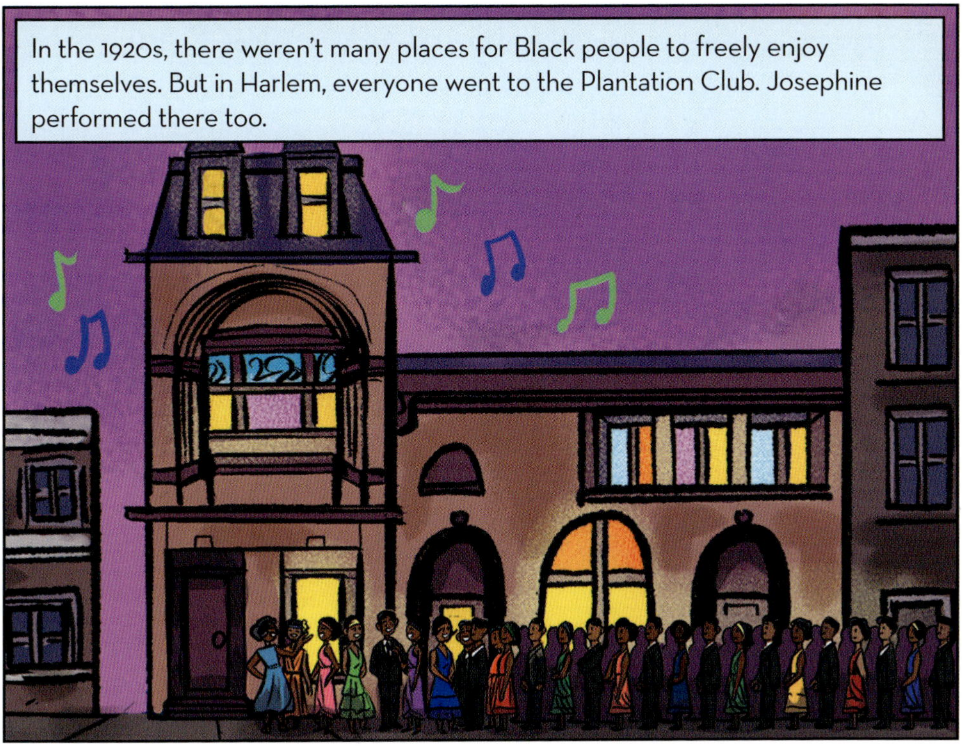
In the 1920s, there weren't many places for Black people to freely enjoy themselves. But in Harlem, everyone went to the Plantation Club. Josephine performed there too.

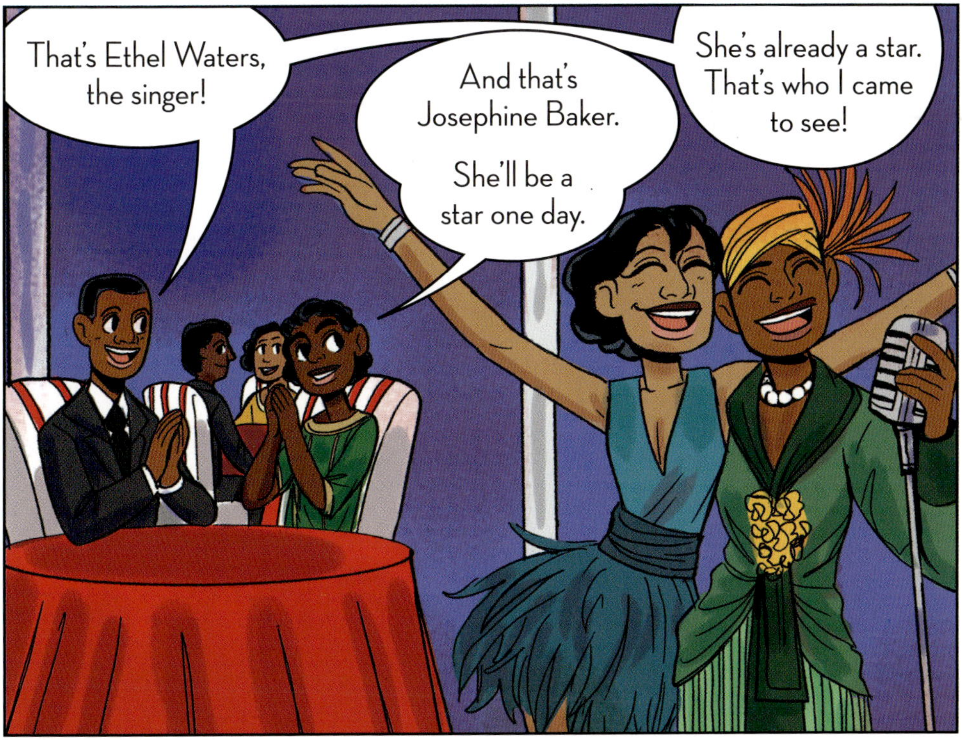
That's Ethel Waters, the singer!
And that's Josephine Baker.
She'll be a star one day.
She's already a star. That's who I came to see!

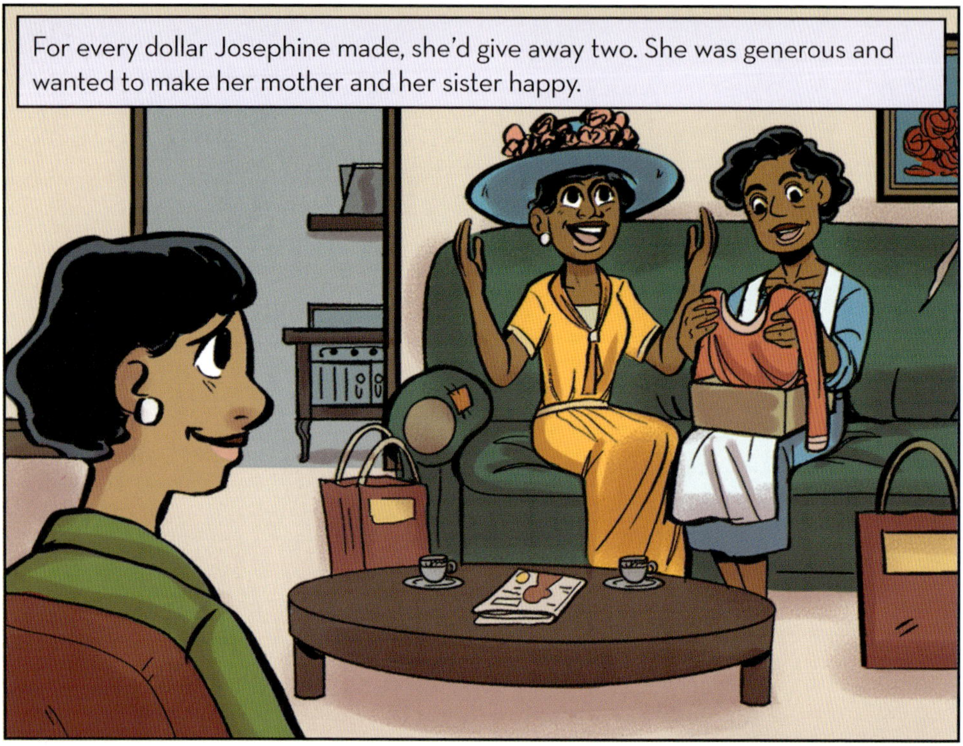
For every dollar Josephine made, she'd give away two. She was generous and wanted to make her mother and her sister happy.

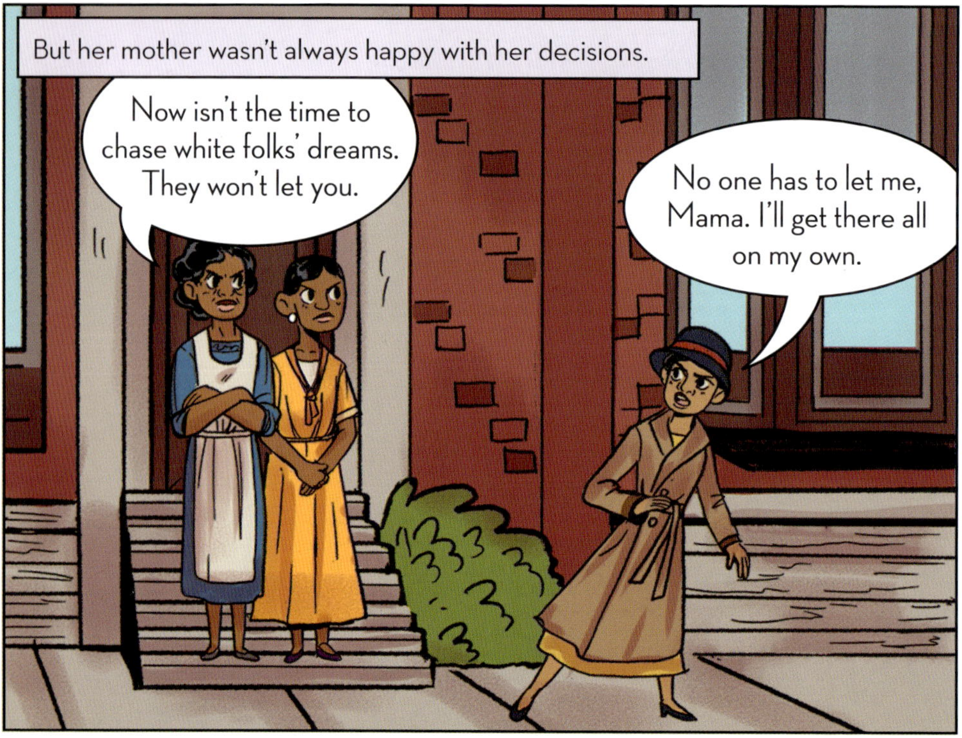
But her mother wasn't always happy with her decisions.
Now isn't the time to chase white folks' dreams. They won't let you.
No one has to let me, Mama. I'll get there all on my own.

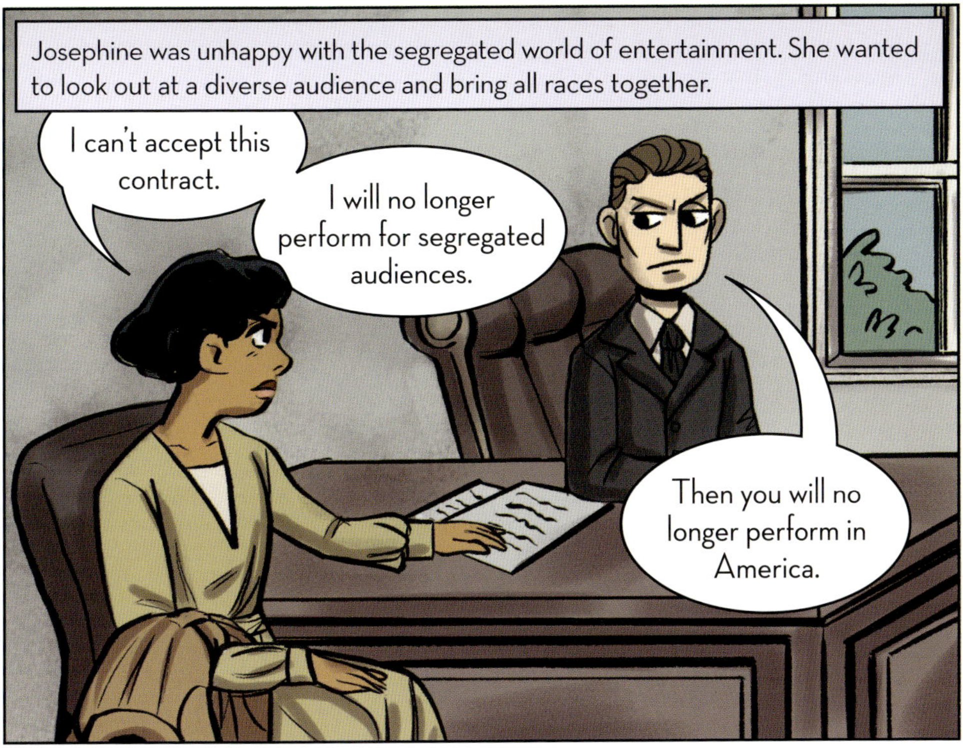
Josephine was unhappy with the segregated world of entertainment. She wanted to look out at a diverse audience and bring all races together.
I can't accept this contract.
I will no longer perform for segregated audiences.
Then you will no longer perform in America.

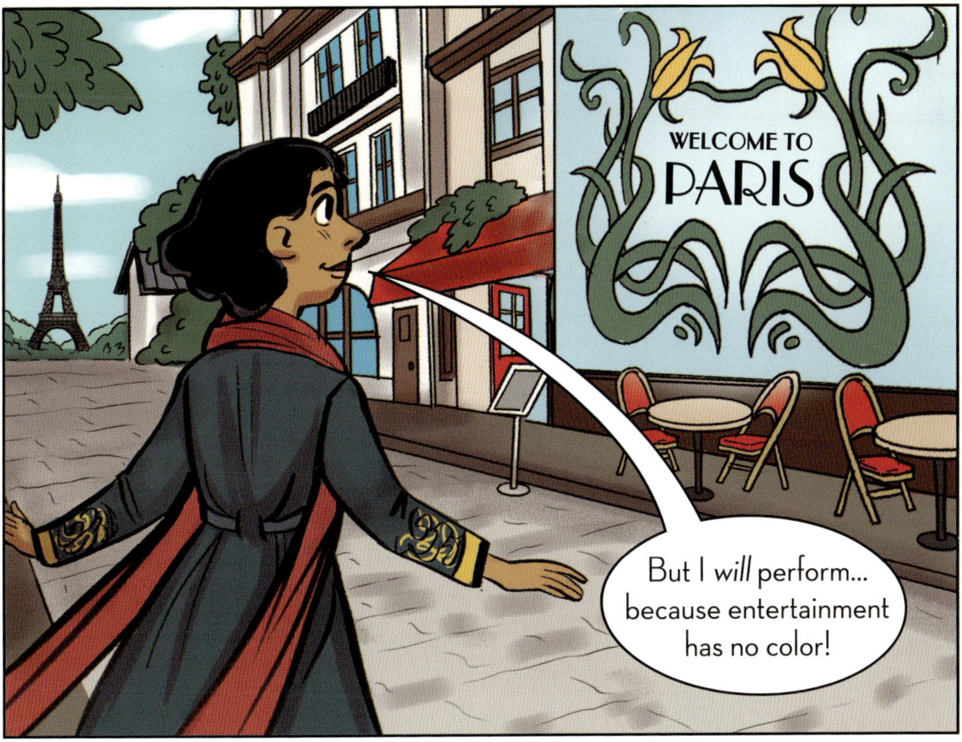
WELCOME TO PARIS
But I *will* perform... because entertainment has no color!

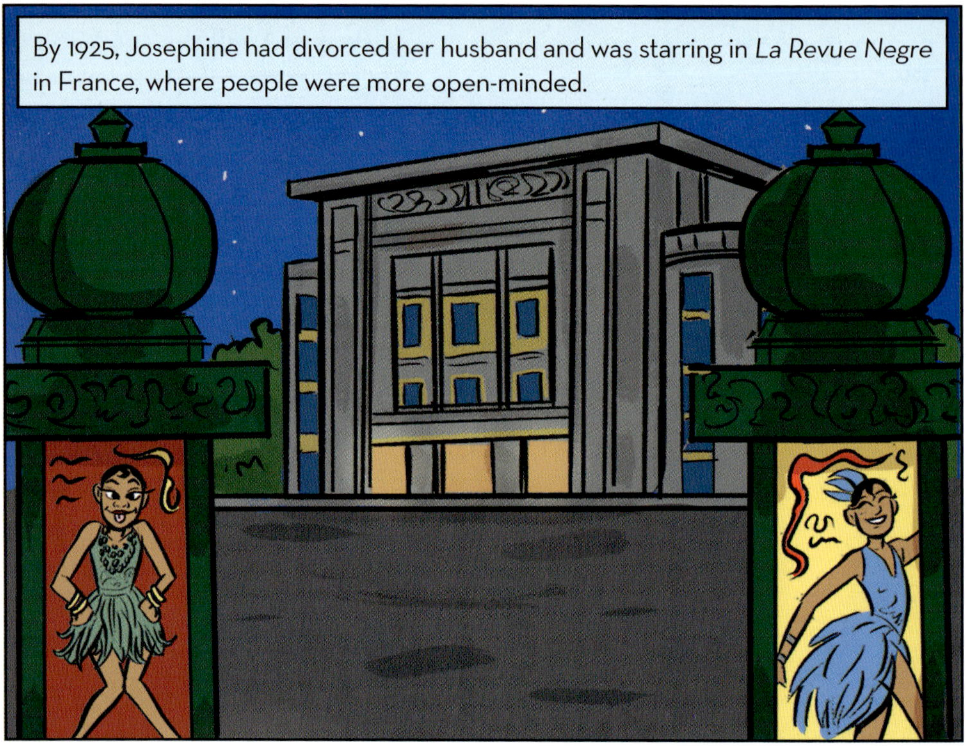
By 1925, Josephine had divorced her husband and was starring in *La Revue Negre* in France, where people were more open-minded.

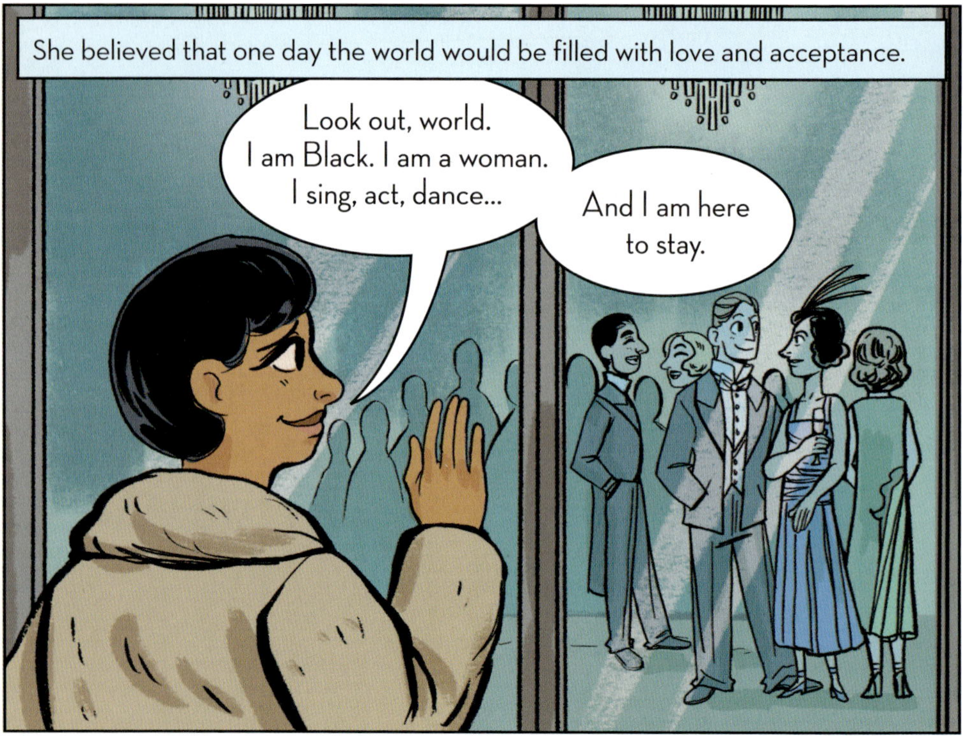
She believed that one day the world would be filled with love and acceptance.
Look out, world. I am Black. I am a woman. I sing, act, dance...
And I am here to stay.

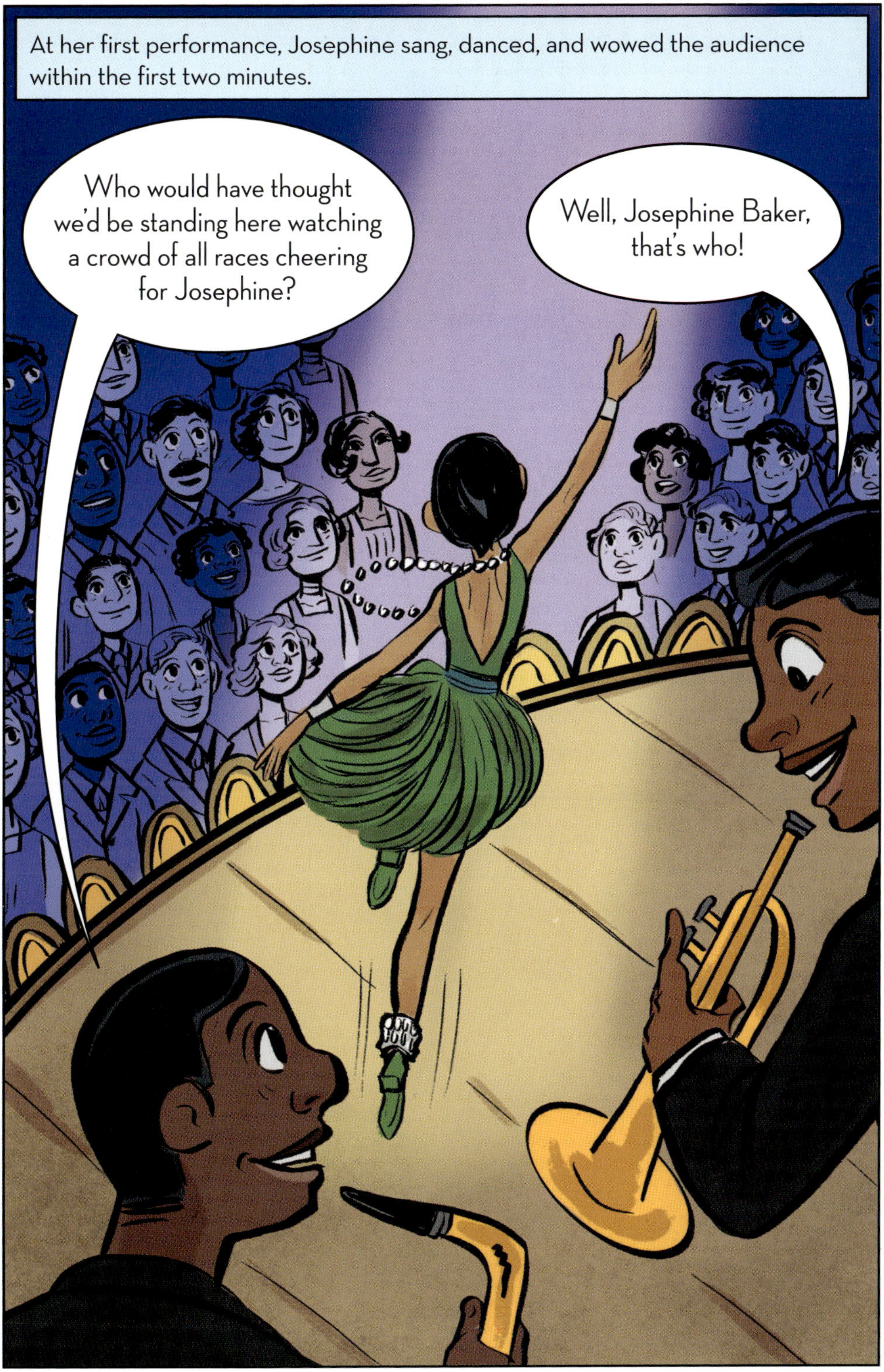
At her first performance, Josephine sang, danced, and wowed the audience within the first two minutes.
Who would have thought we'd be standing here watching a crowd of all races cheering for Josephine?
Well, Josephine Baker, that's who!

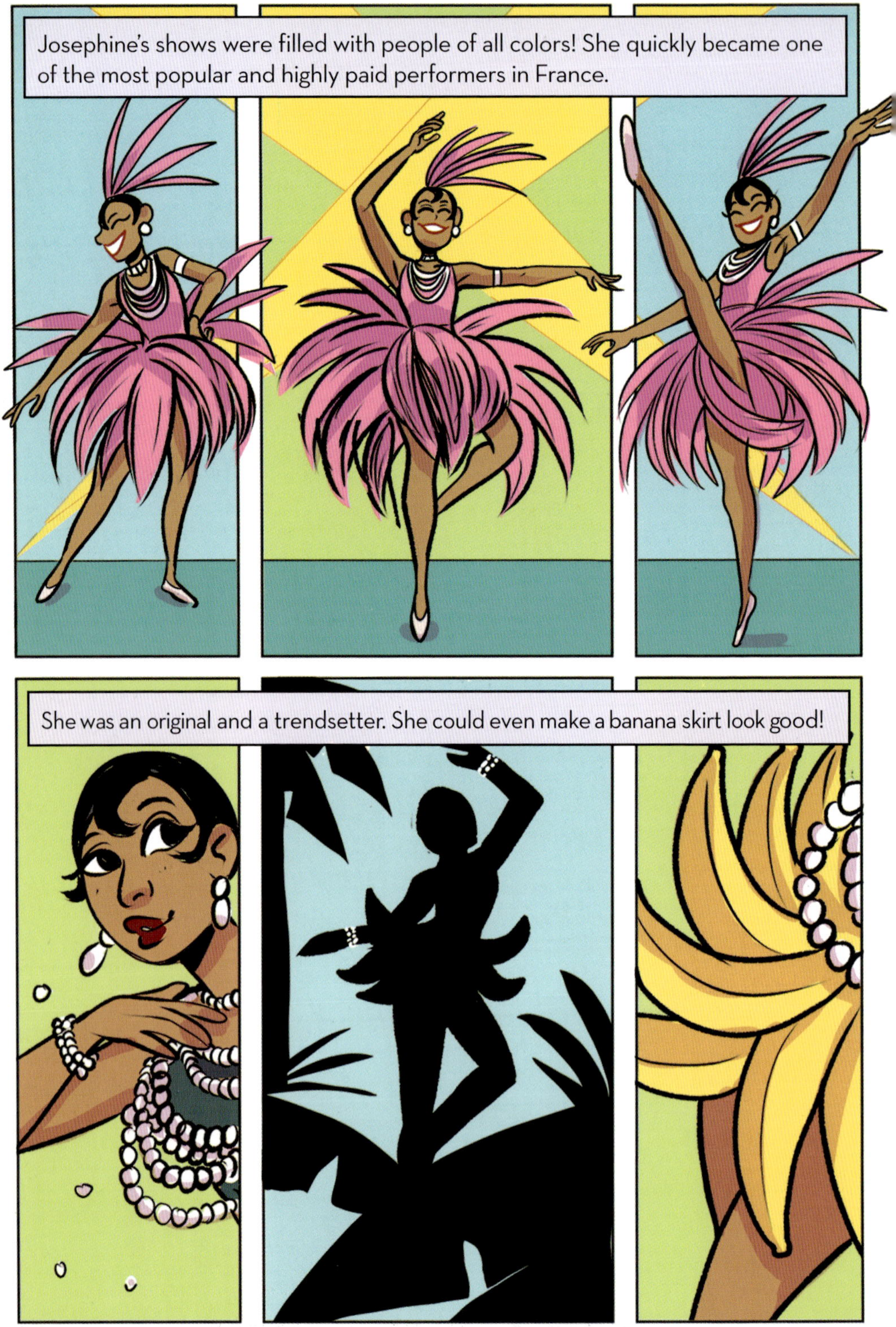
Josephine's shows were filled with people of all colors! She quickly became one of the most popular and highly paid performers in France.
She was an original and a trendsetter. She could even make a banana skirt look good!

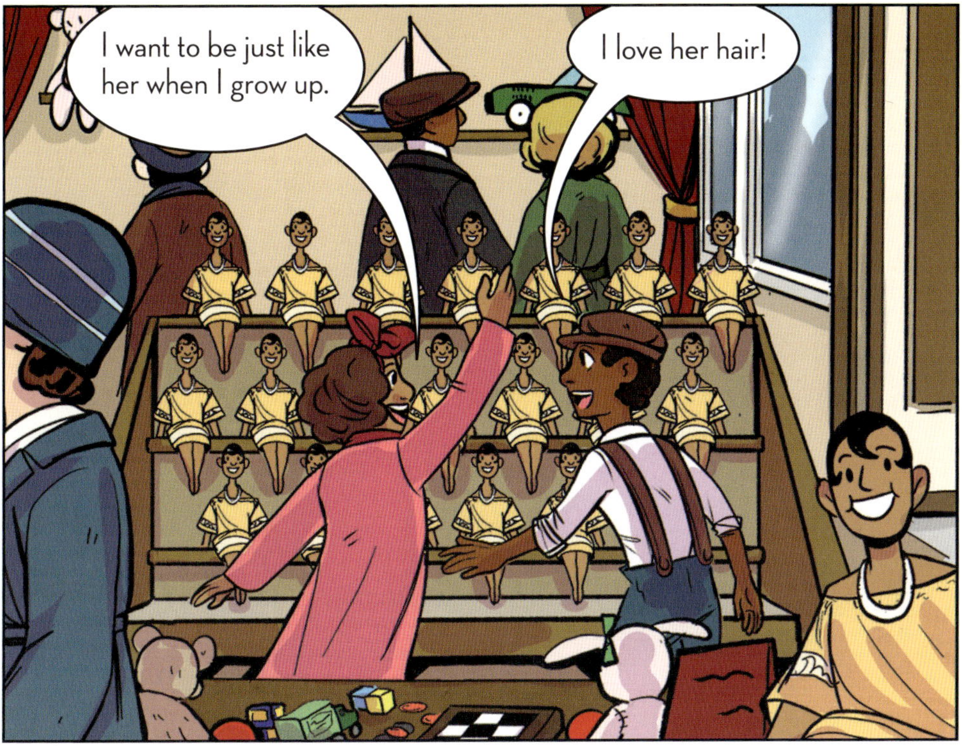
I want to be just like her when I grow up.
I love her hair!

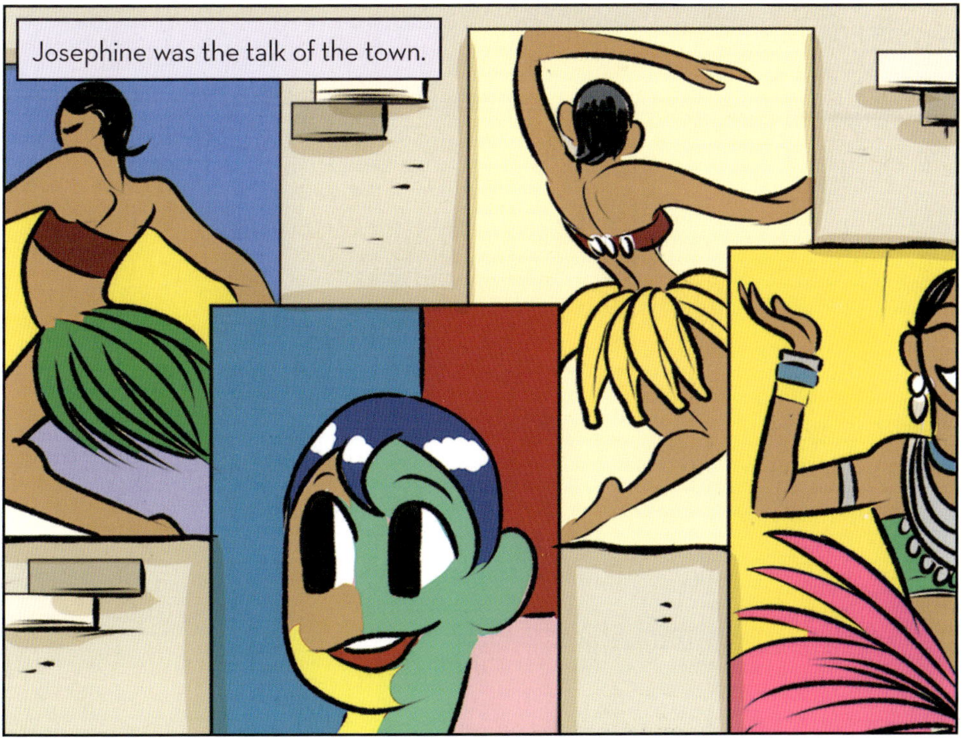
Josephine was the talk of the town.

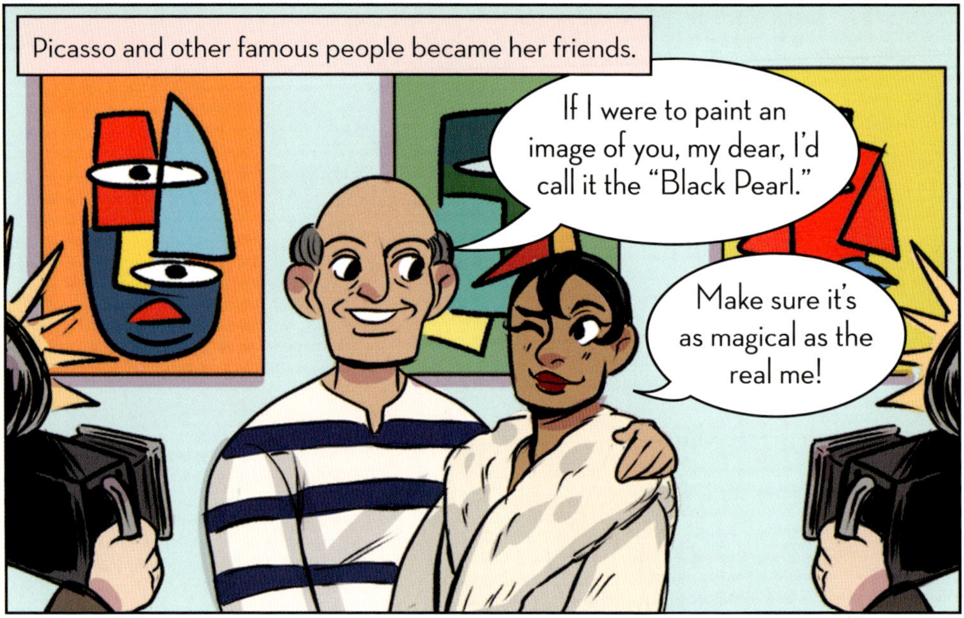
Picasso and other famous people became her friends.
If I were to paint an image of you, my dear, I'd call it the "Black Pearl."
Make sure it's as magical as the real me!

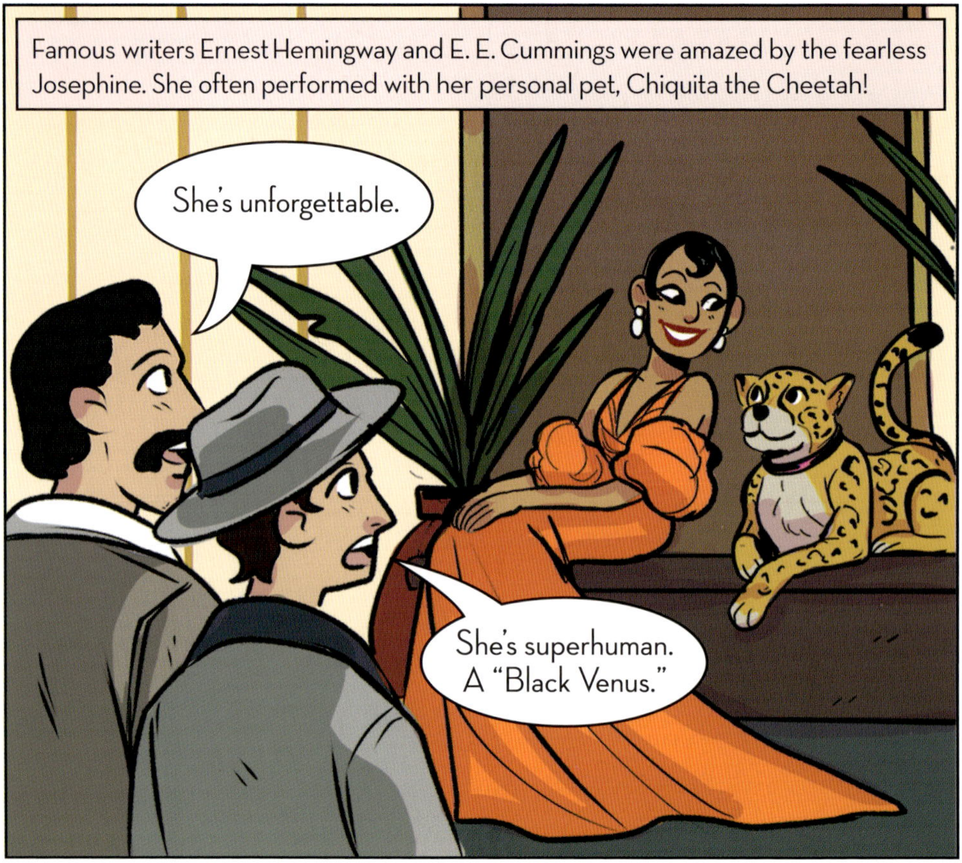
Famous writers Ernest Hemingway and E. E. Cummings were amazed by the fearless Josephine. She often performed with her personal pet, Chiquita the Cheetah!
She's unforgettable.
She's superhuman. A "Black Venus."

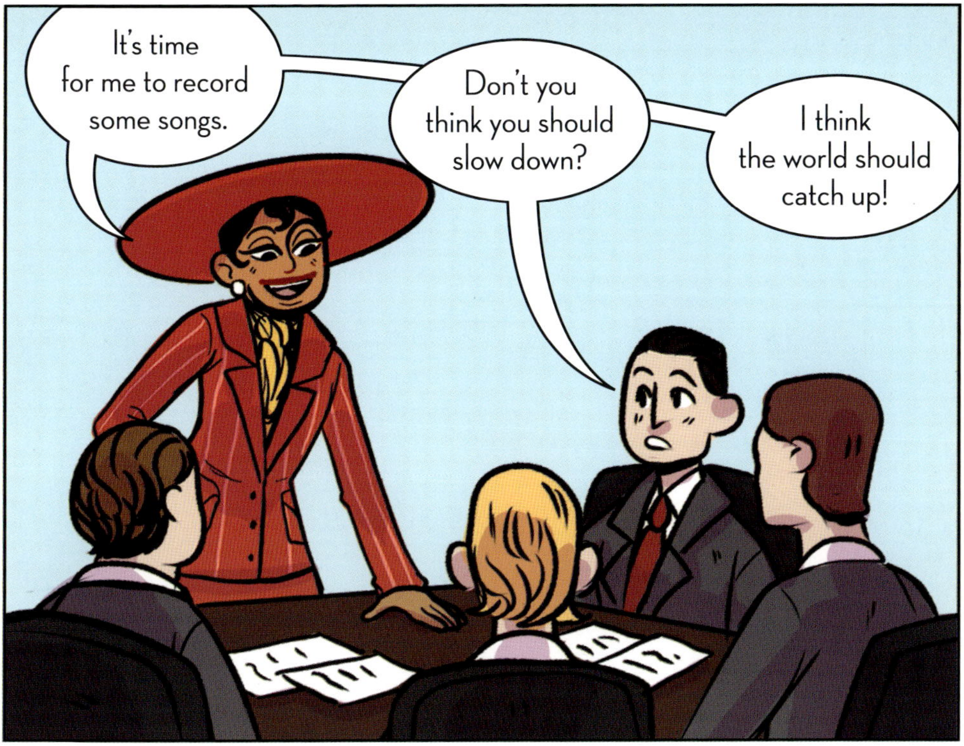
It's time for me to record some songs.
Don't you think you should slow down?
I think the world should catch up!

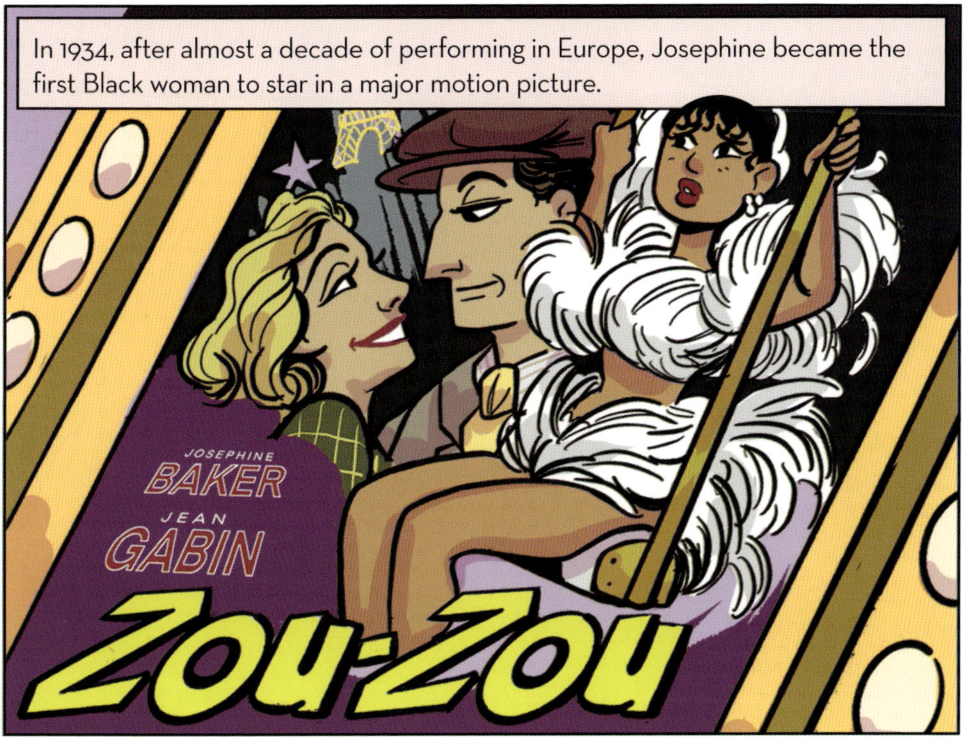
In 1934, after almost a decade of performing in Europe, Josephine became the first Black woman to star in a major motion picture.
JOSEPHINE BAKER
JEAN GABIN
ZOU-ZOU

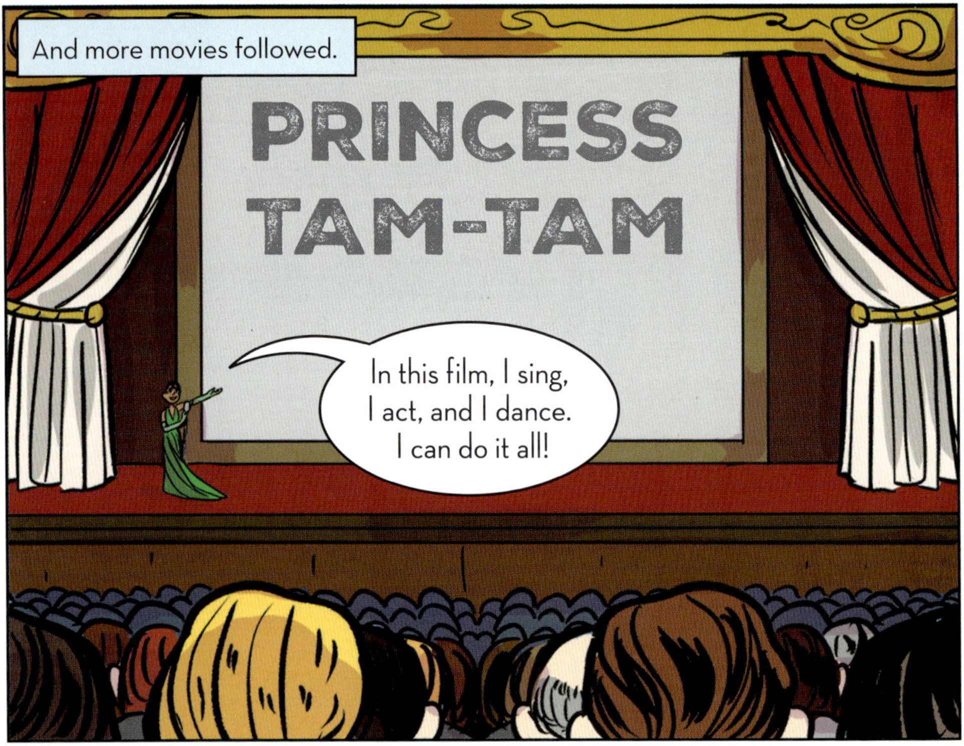
And more movies followed.
PRINCESS TAM-TAM
In this film, I sing, I act, and I dance. I can do it all!

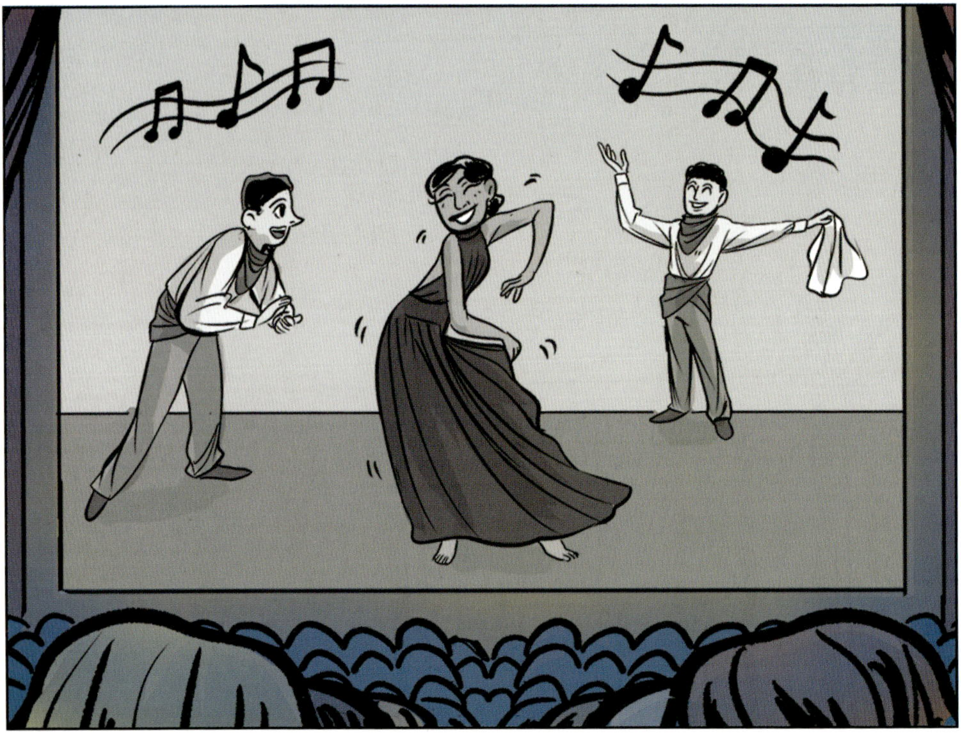

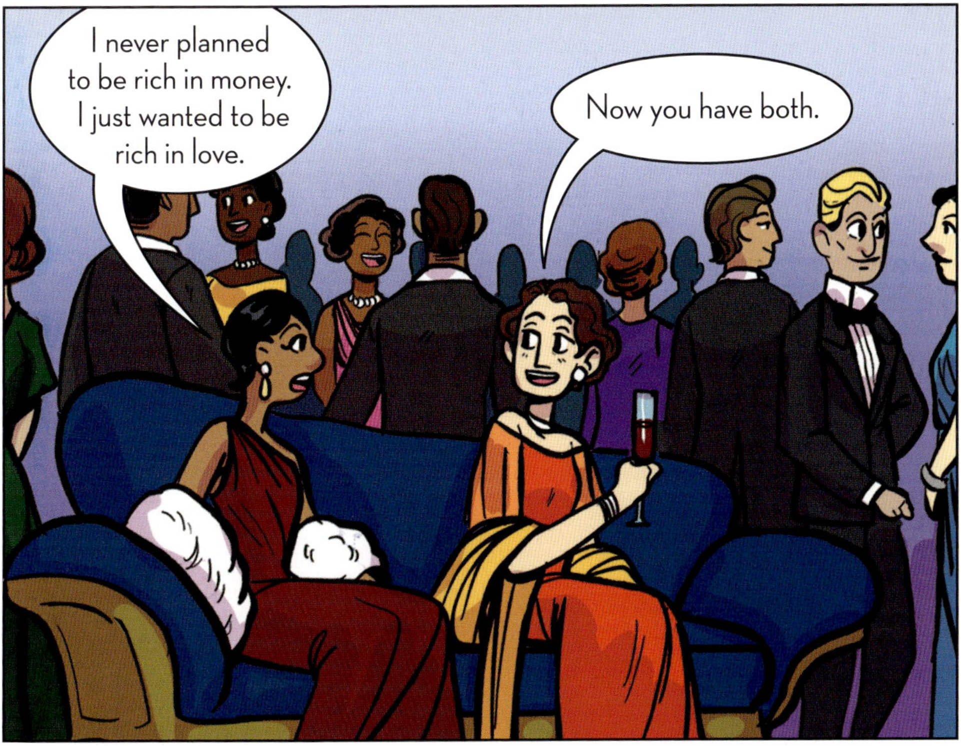
I never planned to be rich in money. I just wanted to be rich in love.
Now you have both.

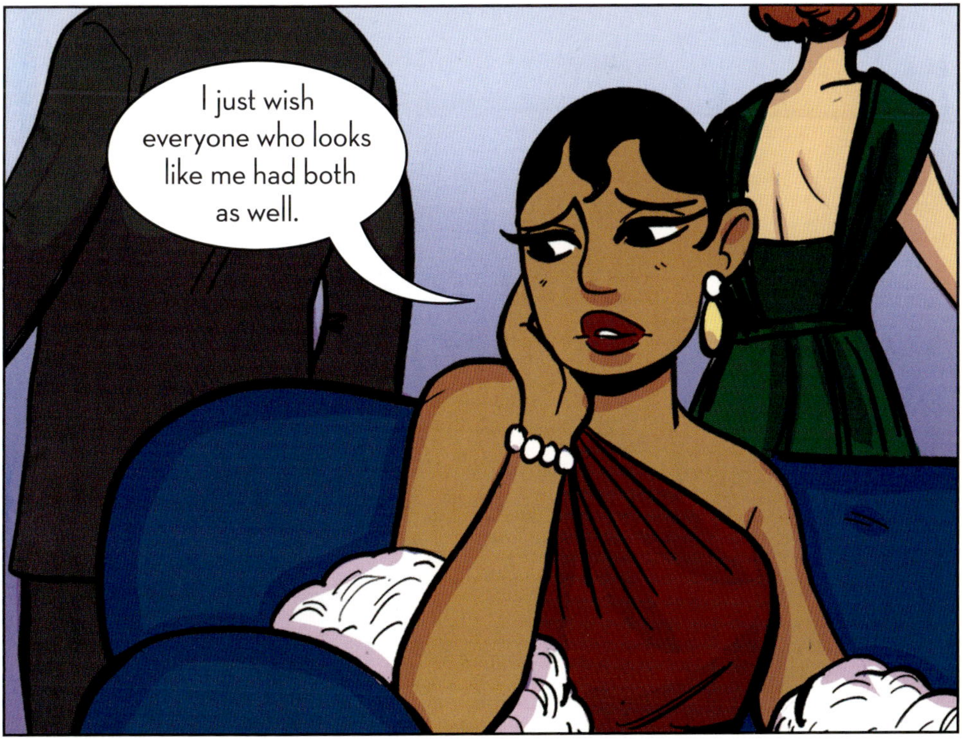
I just wish everyone who looks like me had both as well.

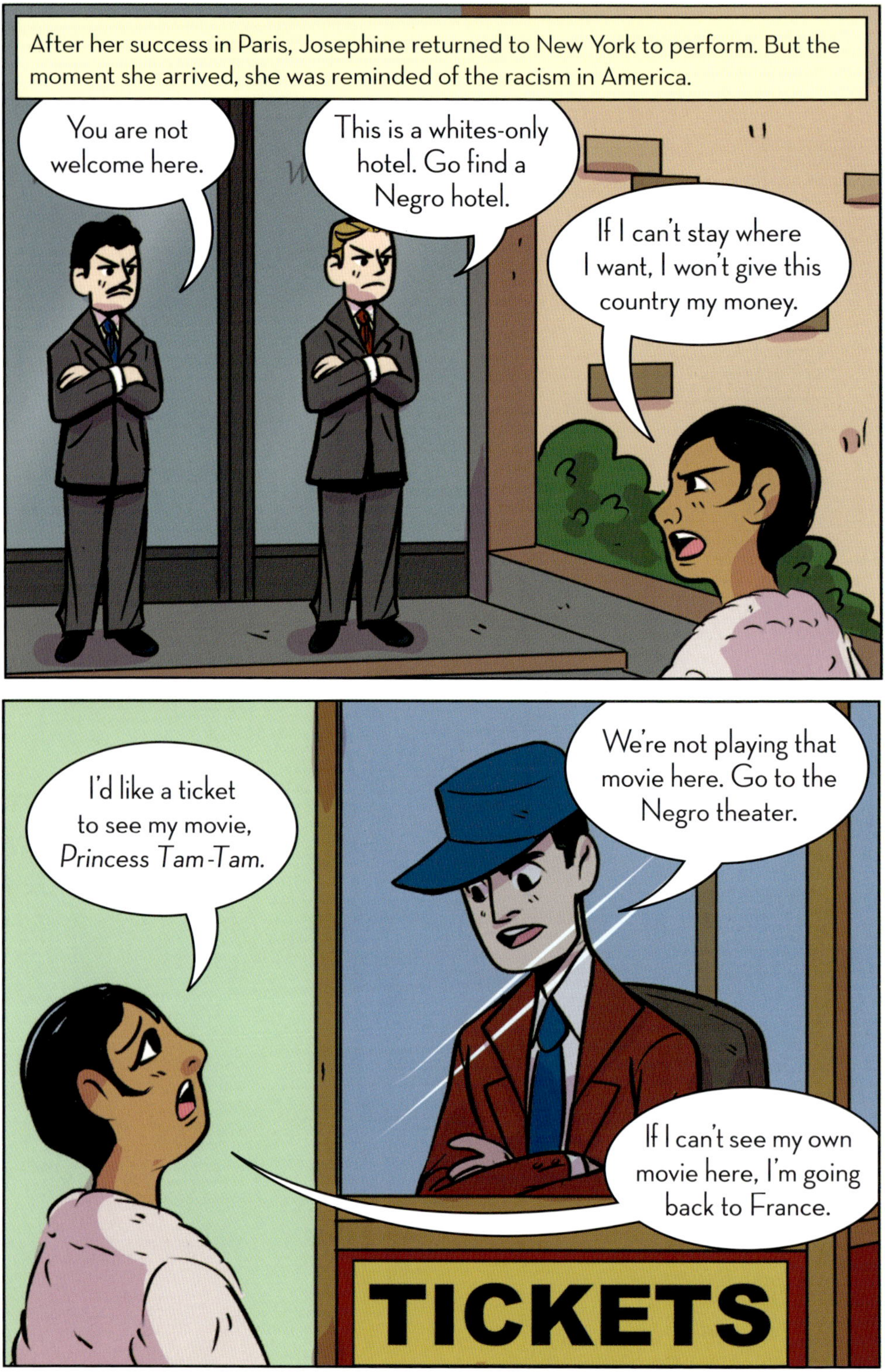
After her success in Paris, Josephine returned to New York to perform. But the moment she arrived, she was reminded of the racism in America.
You are not welcome here.
This is a whites-only hotel. Go find a Negro hotel.
If I can't stay where I want, I won't give this country my money.
I'd like a ticket to see my movie, *Princess Tam-Tam.*
We're not playing that movie here. Go to the Negro theater.
If I can't see my own movie here, I'm going back to France.
TICKETS

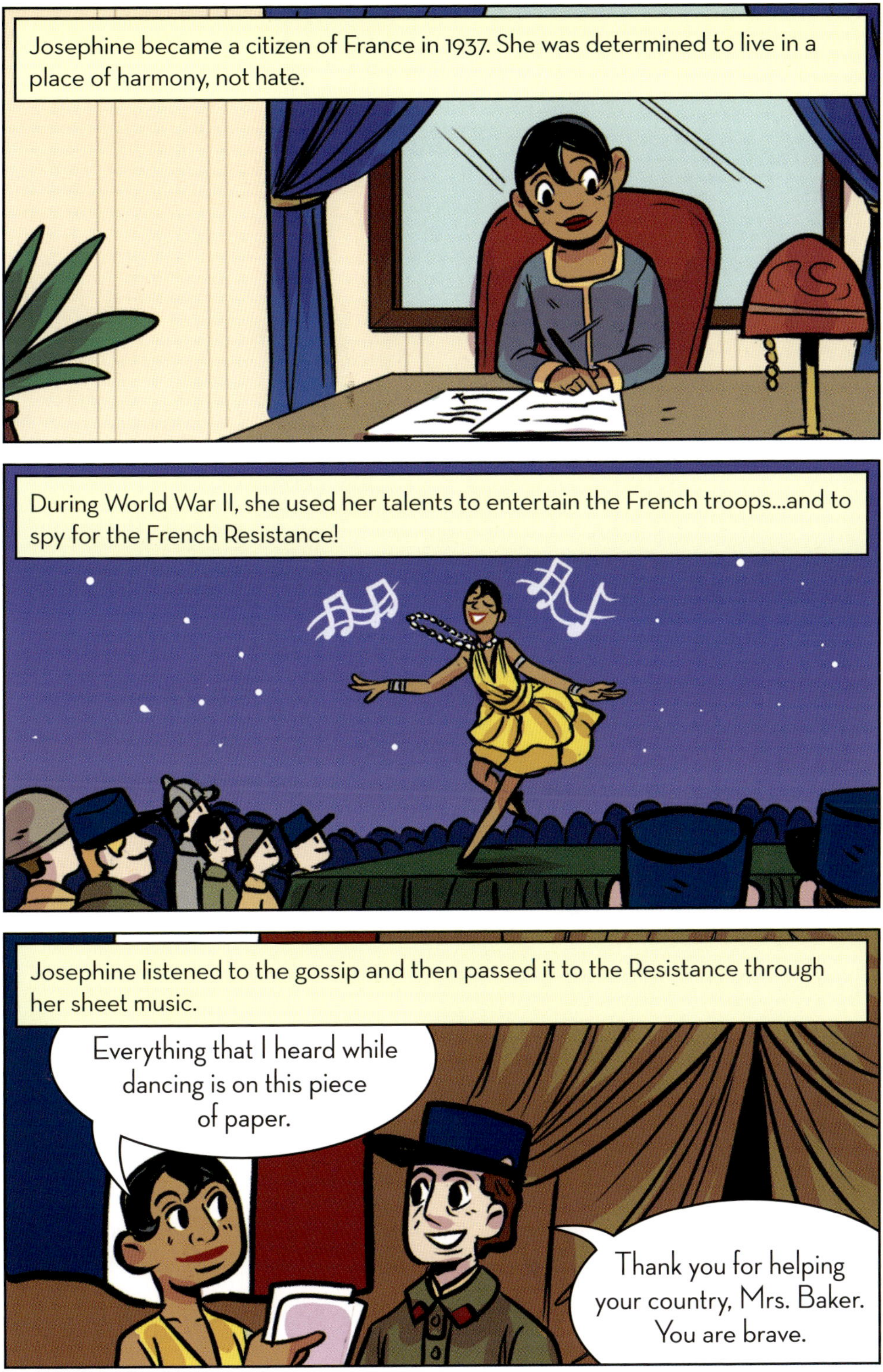
Josephine became a citizen of France in 1937. She was determined to live in a place of harmony, not hate.
During World War II, she used her talents to entertain the French troops...and to spy for the French Resistance!
Josephine listened to the gossip and then passed it to the Resistance through her sheet music.
Everything that I heard while dancing is on this piece of paper.
Thank you for helping your country, Mrs. Baker. You are brave.

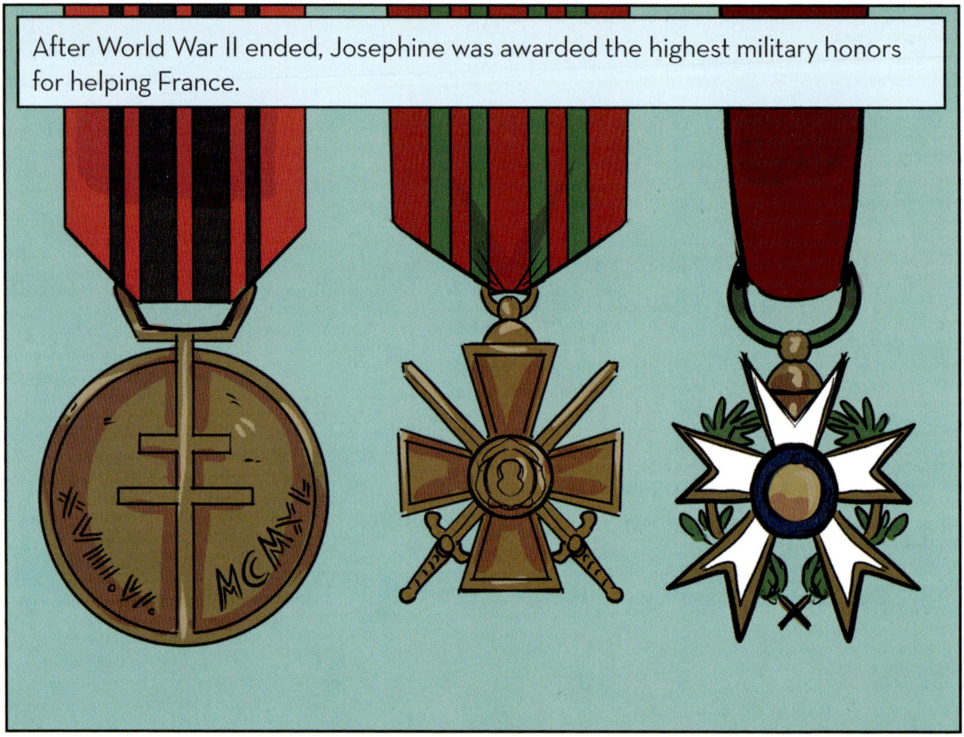
After World War II ended, Josephine was awarded the highest military honors for helping France.
MCM

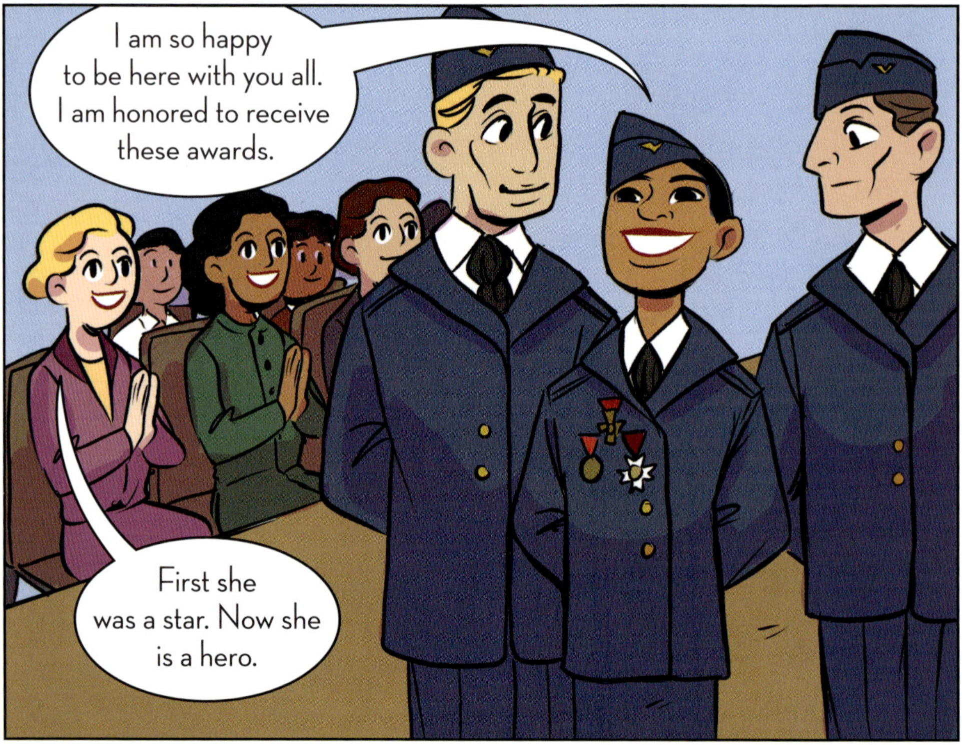
I am so happy to be here with you all. I am honored to receive these awards.
First she was a star. Now she is a hero.

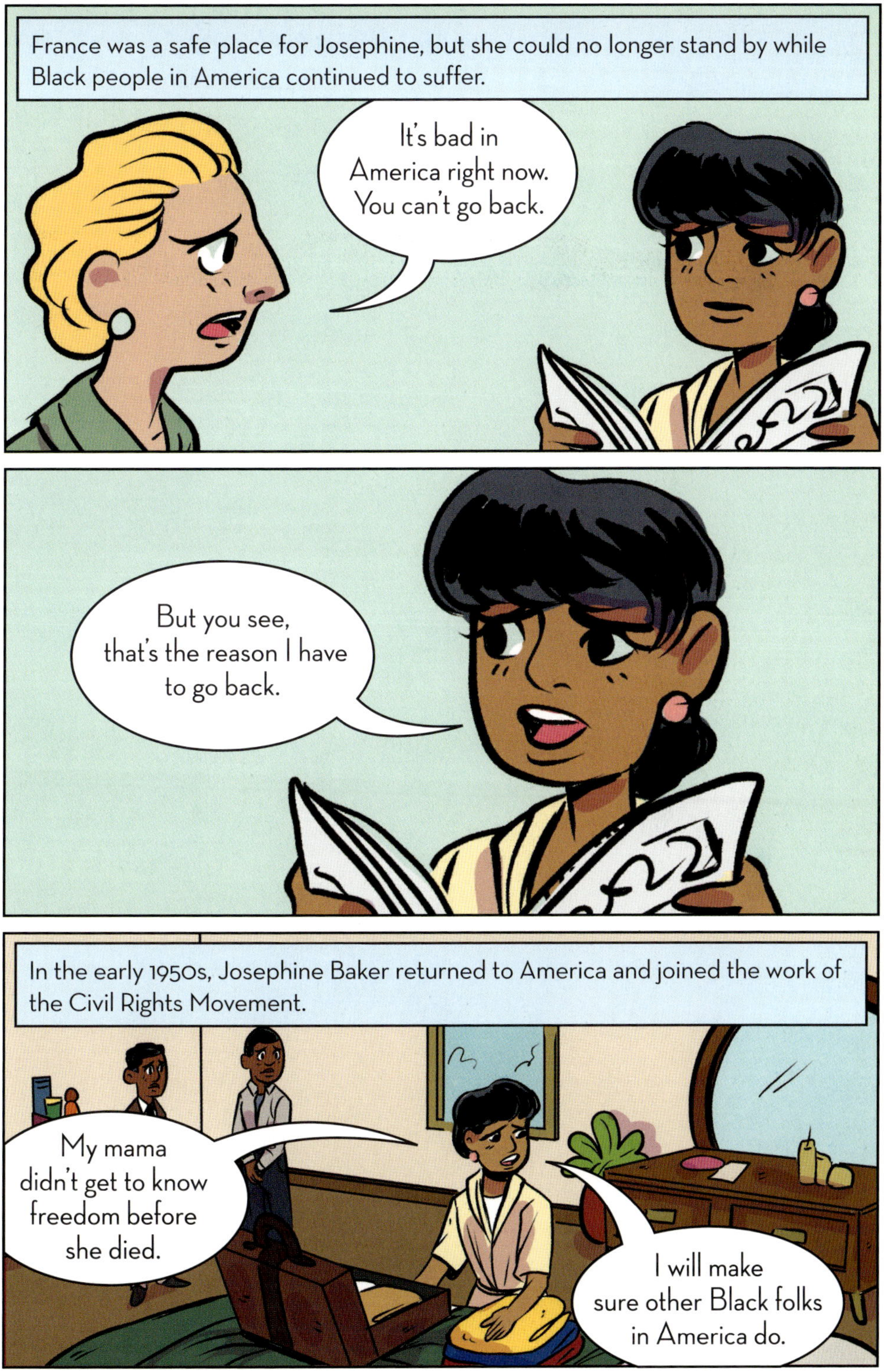
France was a safe place for Josephine, but she could no longer stand by while Black people in America continued to suffer.
It's bad in America right now. You can't go back.
But you see, that's the reason I have to go back.
In the early 1950s, Josephine Baker returned to America and joined the work of the Civil Rights Movement.
My mama didn't get to know freedom before she died.
I will make sure other Black folks in America do.

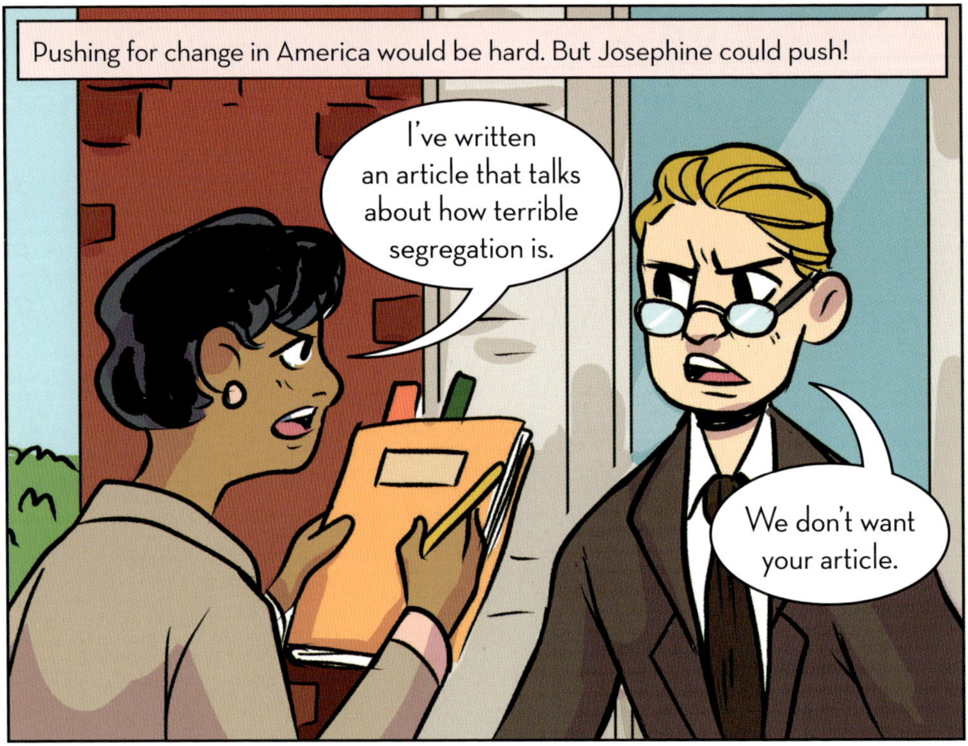
Pushing for change in America would be hard. But Josephine could push!
I've written an article that talks about how terrible segregation is.
We don't want your article.

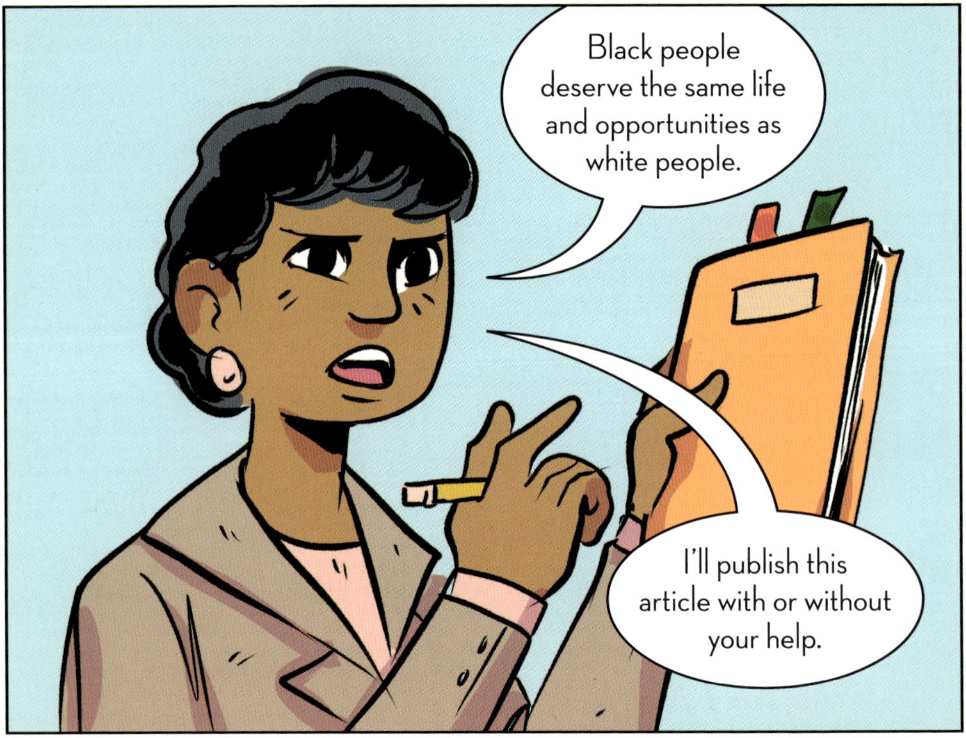
Black people deserve the same life and opportunities as white people.
I'll publish this article with or without your help.

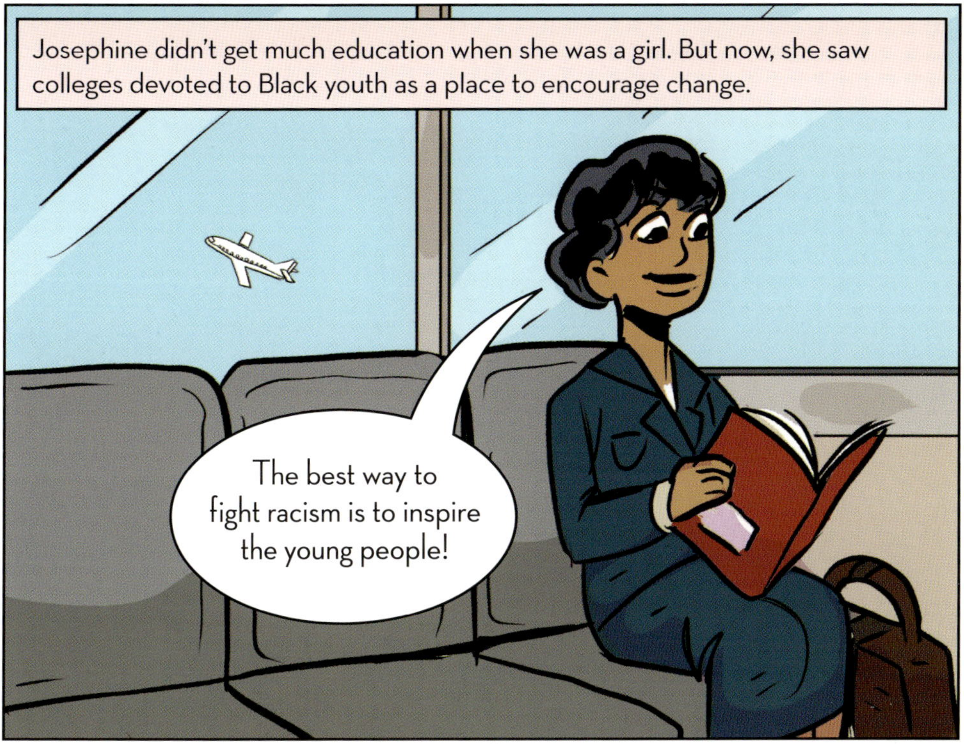
Josephine didn't get much education when she was a girl. But now, she saw colleges devoted to Black youth as a place to encourage change.
The best way to fight racism is to inspire the young people!

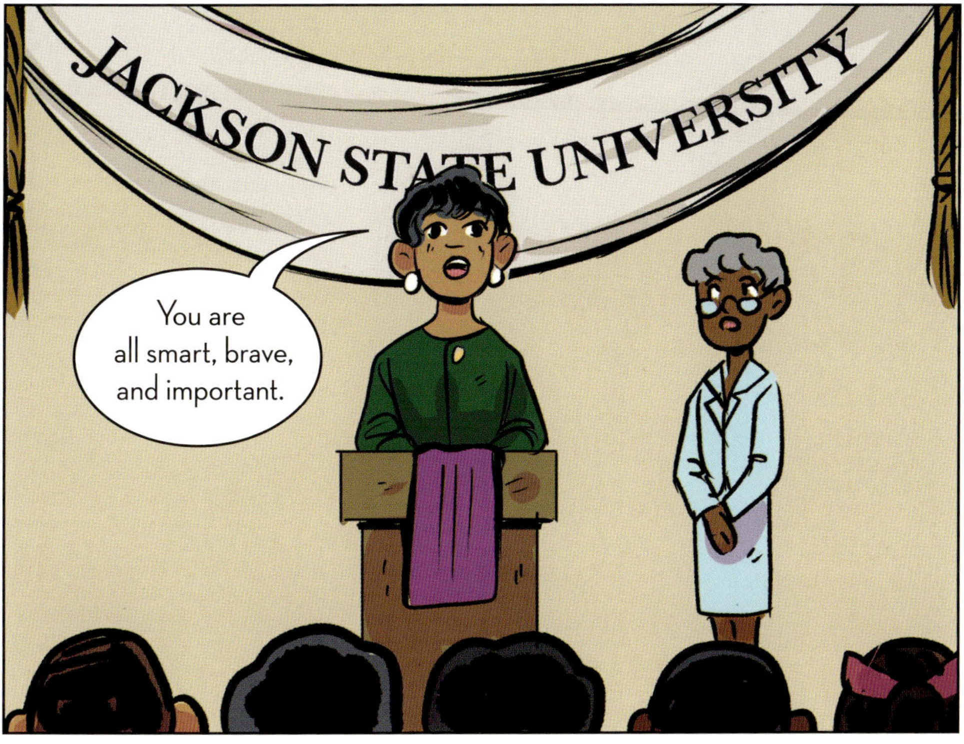
JACKSON STATE UNIVERSTTY
You are all smart, brave, and important.

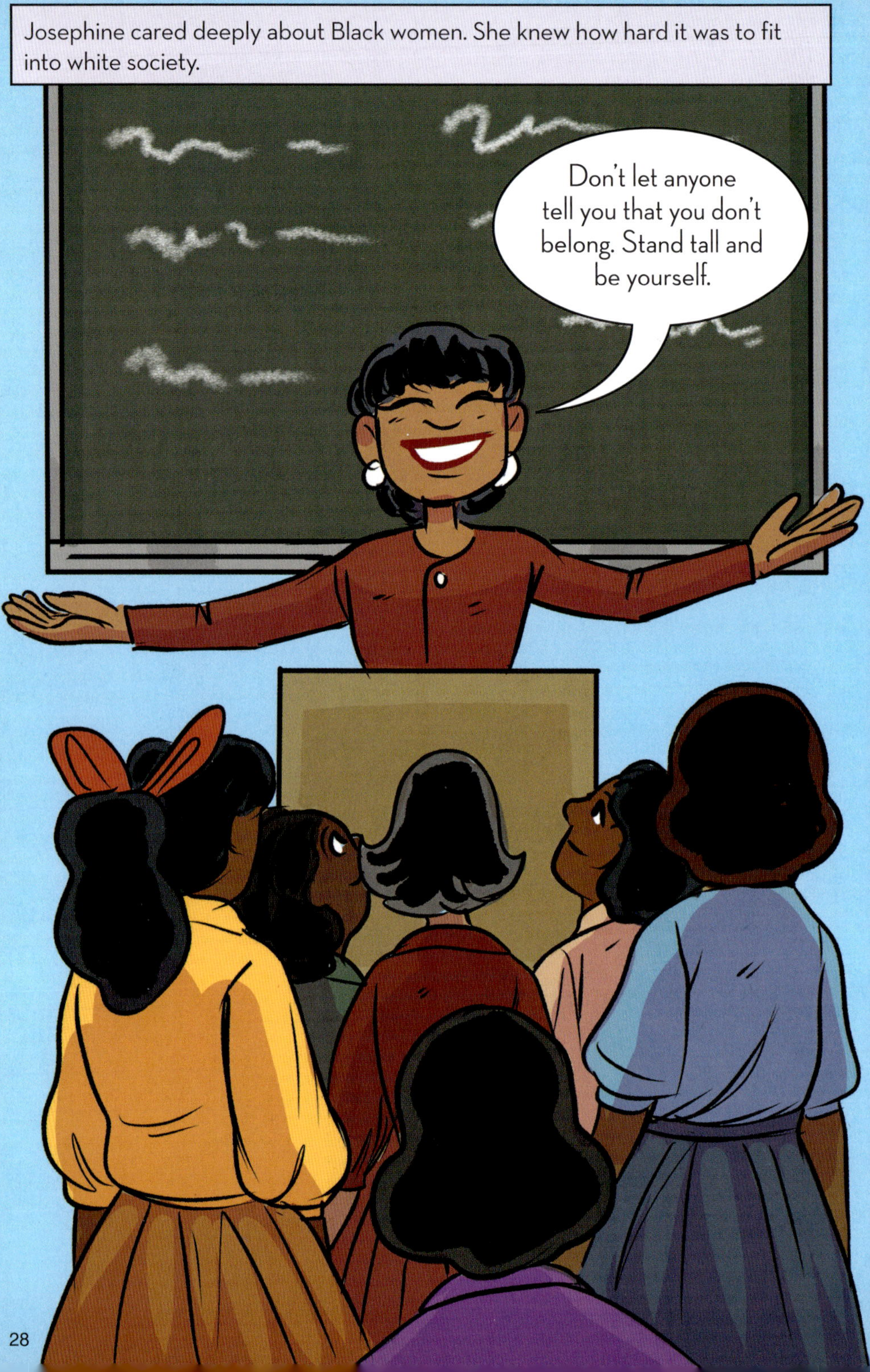
Josephine cared deeply about Black women. She knew how hard it was to fit into white society.
Don't let anyone tell you that you don't belong. Stand tall and be yourself.

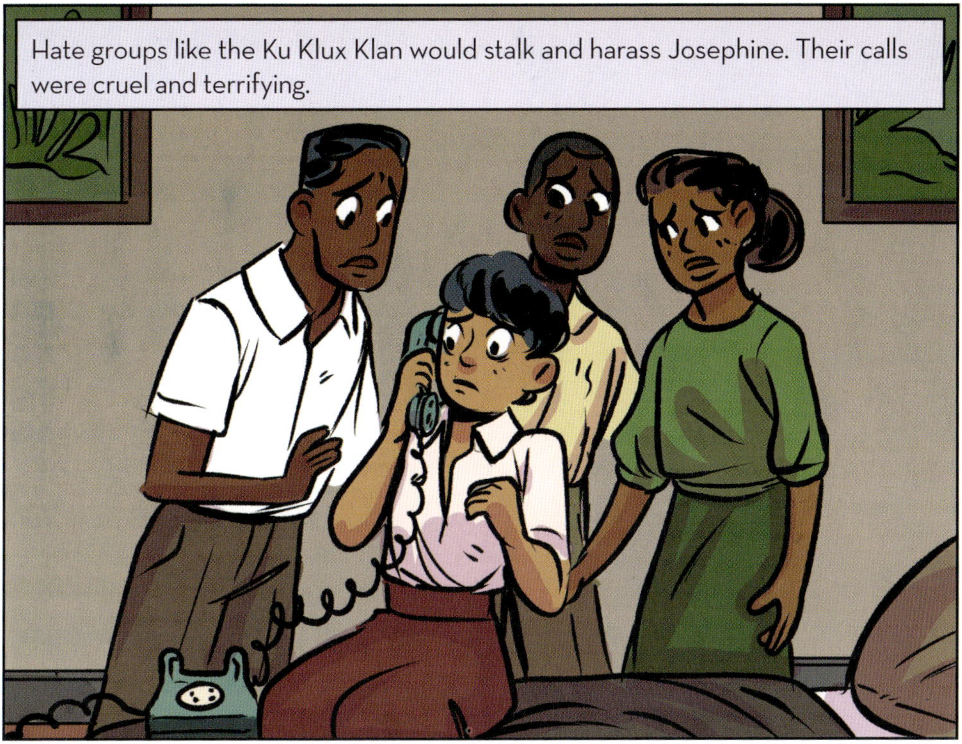
Hate groups like the Ku Klux Klan would stalk and harass Josephine. Their calls were cruel and terrifying.

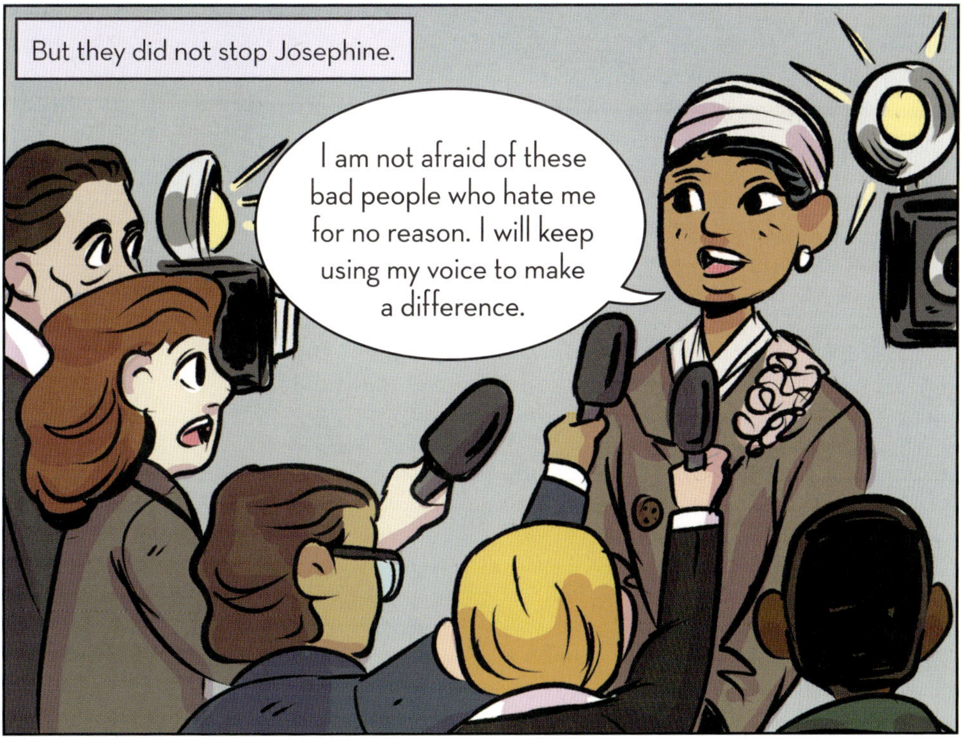
But they did not stop Josephine.
I am not afraid of these bad people who hate me for no reason. I will keep using my voice to make a difference.

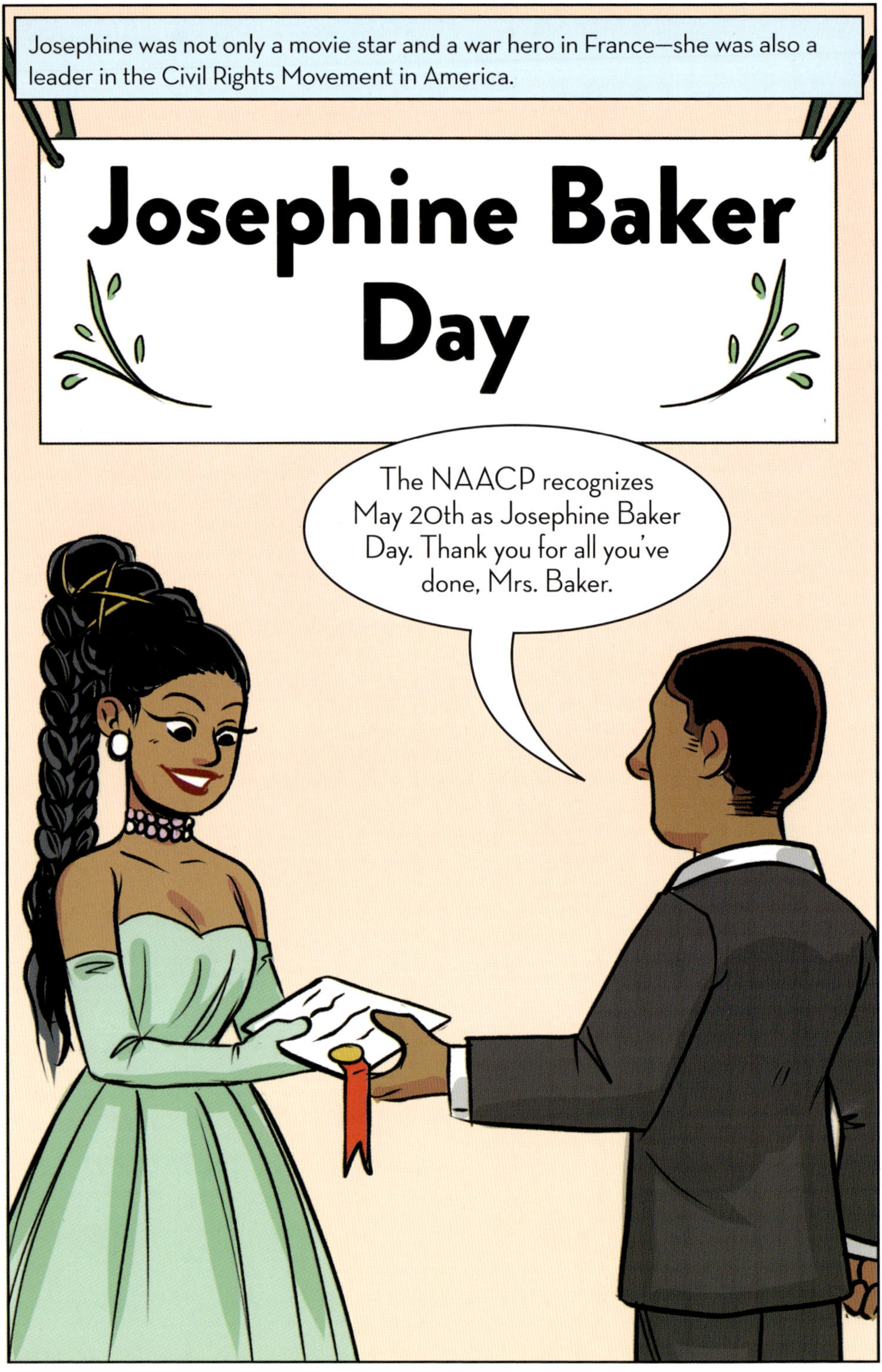
Josephine was not only a movie star and a war hero in France—she was also a leader in the Civil Rights Movement in America.
Josephine Baker Day
The NAACP recognizes May 20th as Josephine Baker Day. Thank you for all you've done, Mrs. Baker.

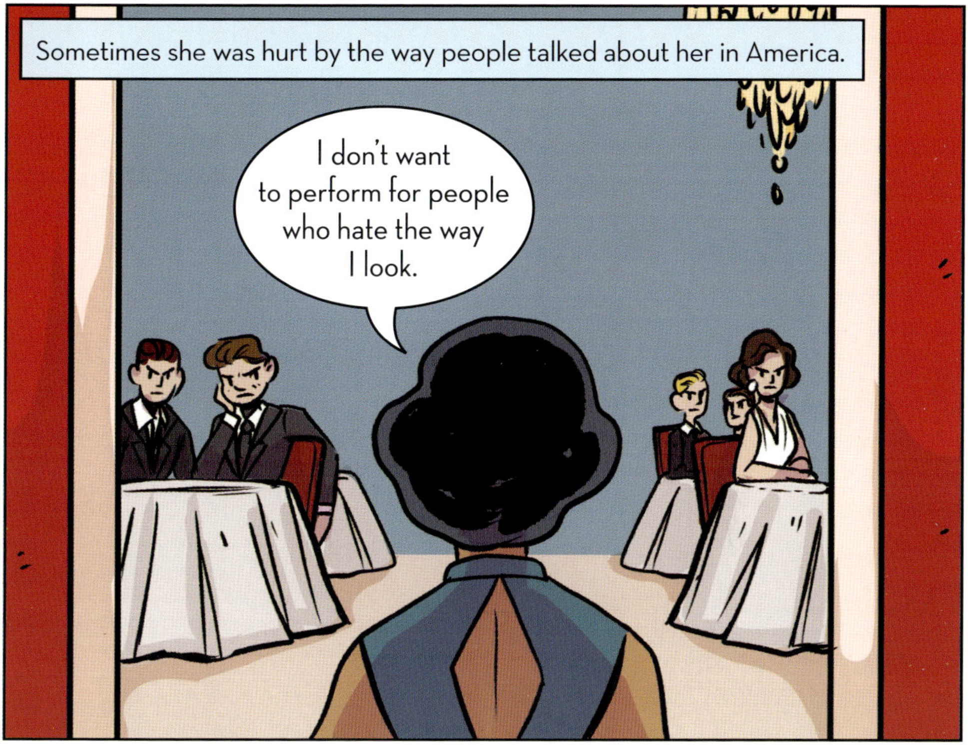
Sometimes she was hurt by the way people talked about her in America.
I don't want to perform for people who hate the way I look.

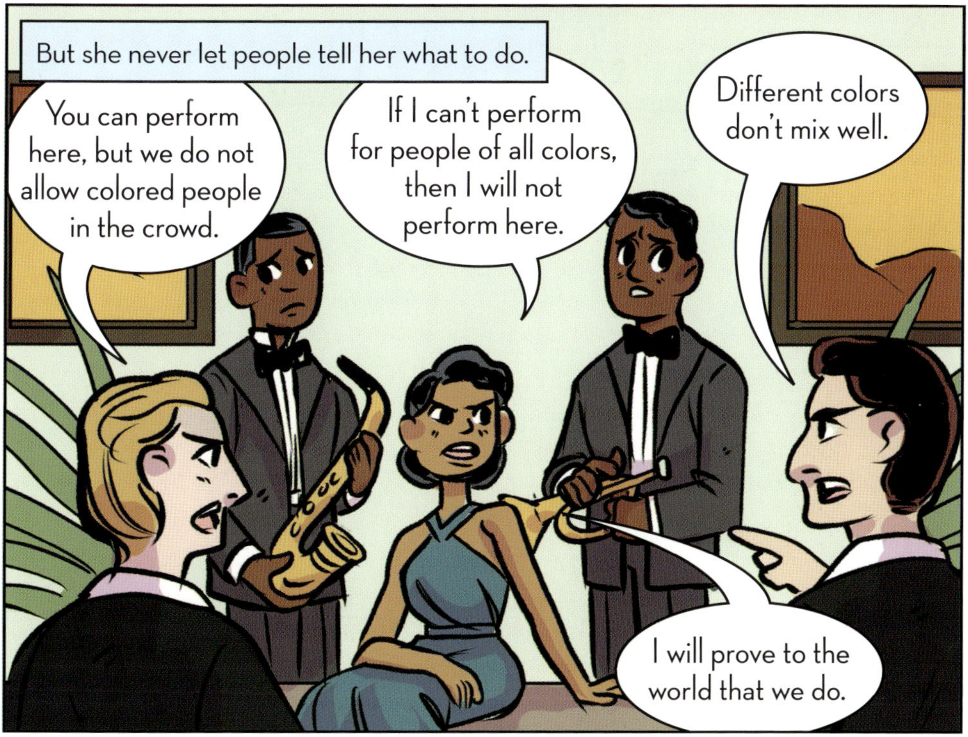
But she never let people tell her what to do.
You can perform here, but we do not allow colored people in the crowd.
If I can't perform for people of all colors, then I will not perform here.
Different colors don't mix well.
I will prove to the world that we do.

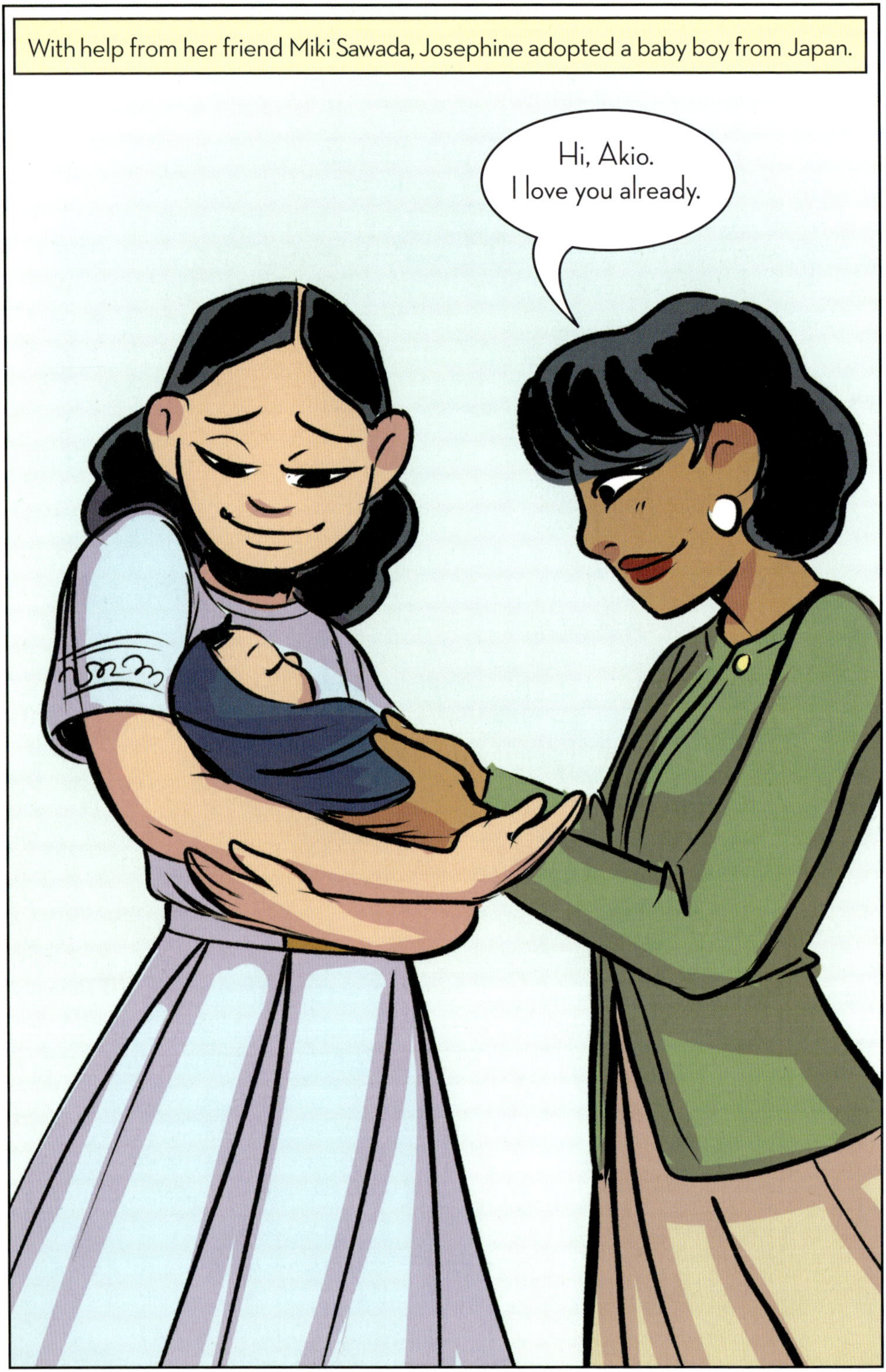
With help from her friend Miki Sawada, Josephine adopted a baby boy from Japan.
Hi, Akio. I love you already.

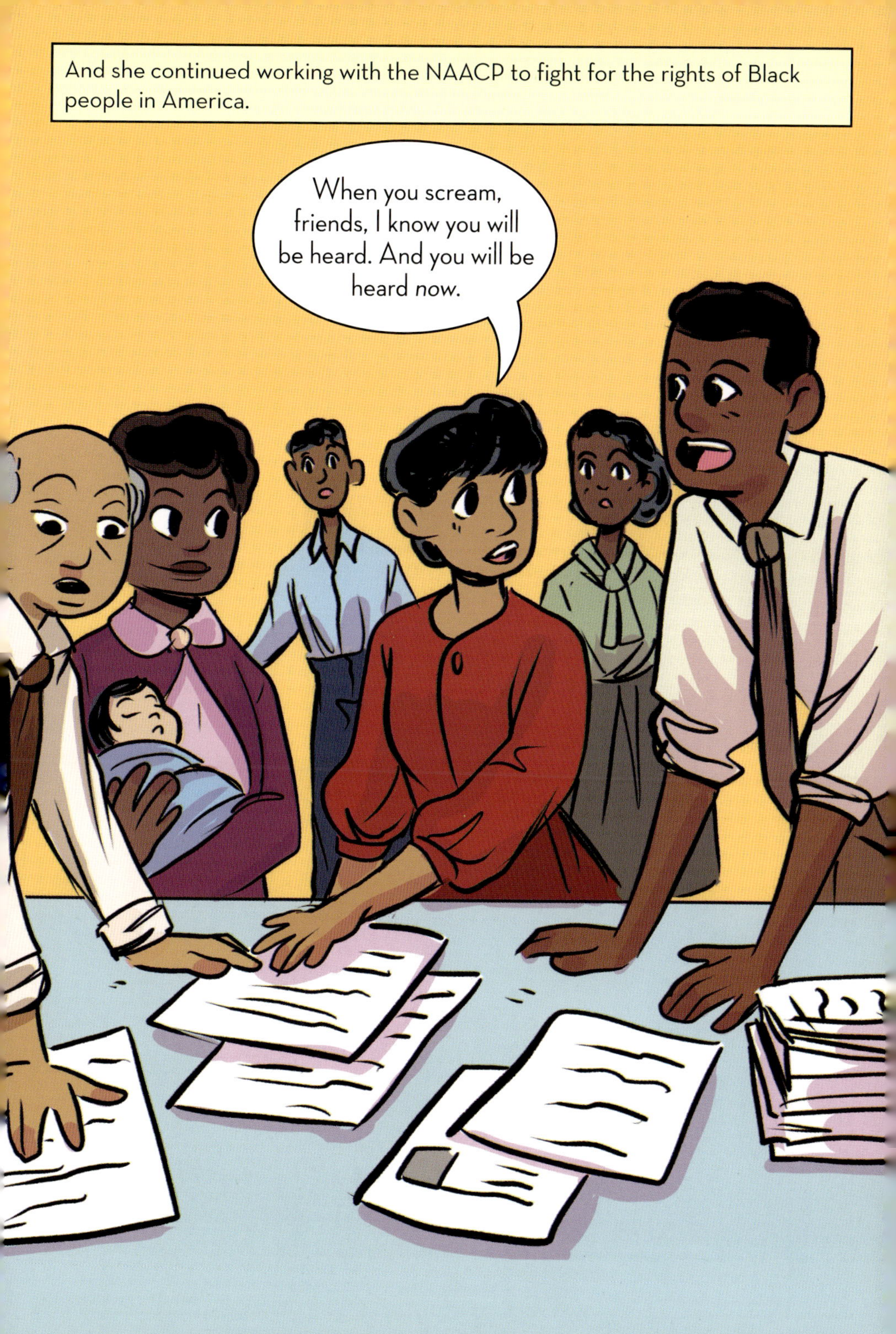
And she continued working with the NAACP to fight for the rights of Black people in America.
When you scream, friends, I know you will be heard. And you will be heard *now*.

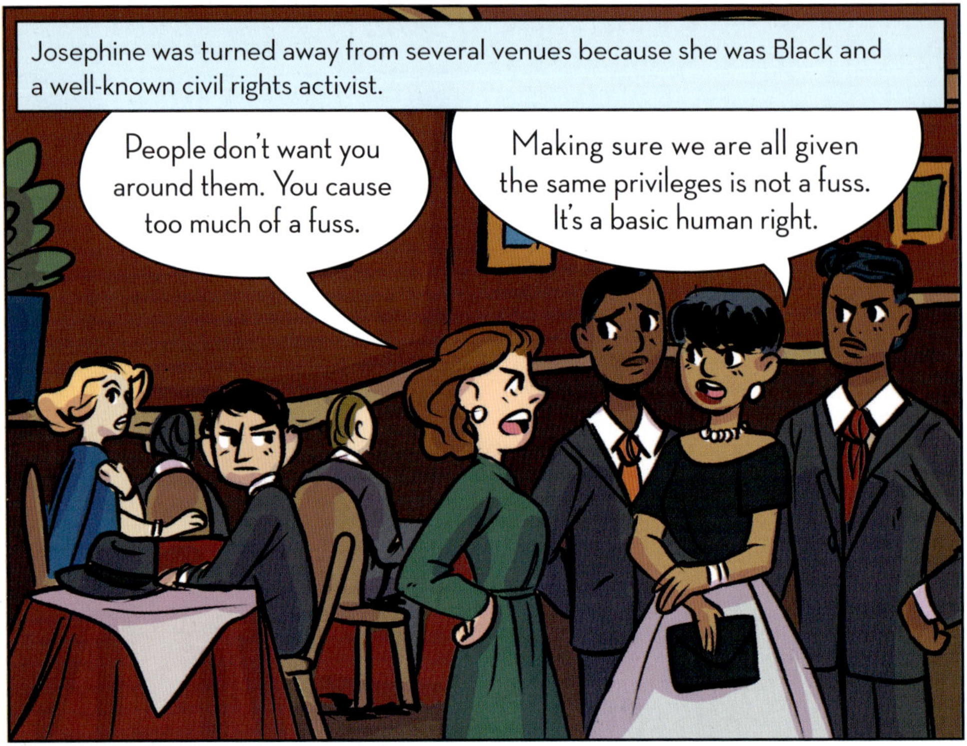
Josephine was turned away from several venues because she was Black and a well-known civil rights activist.
People don't want you around them. You cause too much of a fuss.
Making sure we are all given the same privileges is not a fuss. It's a basic human right.

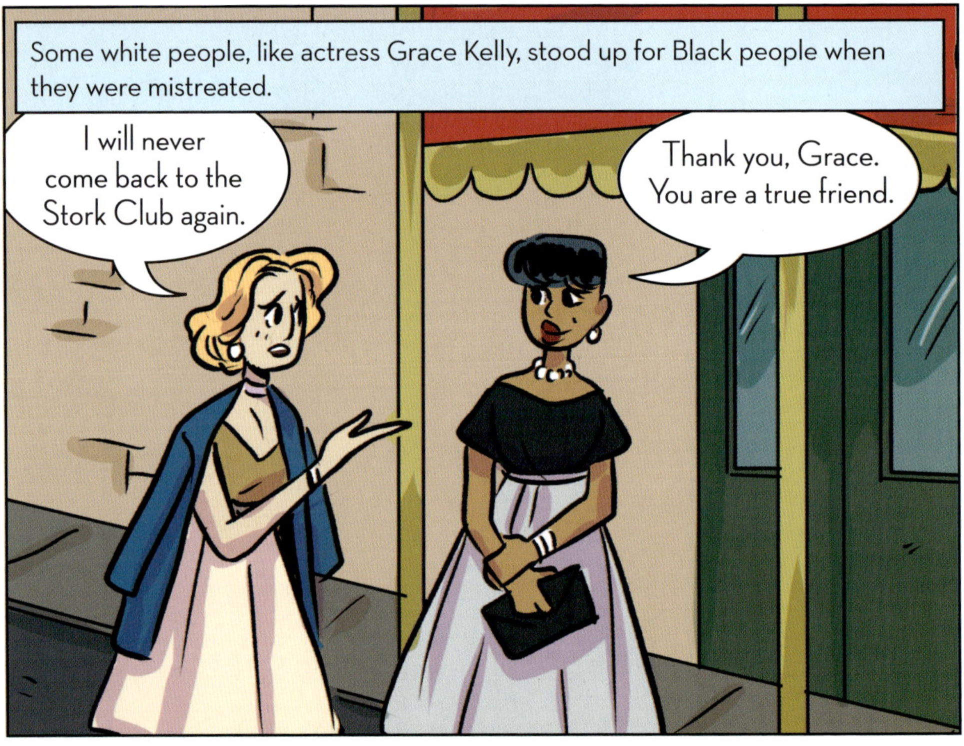
Some white people, like actress Grace Kelly, stood up for Black people when they were mistreated.
I will never come back to the Stork Club again.
Thank you, Grace. You are a true friend.

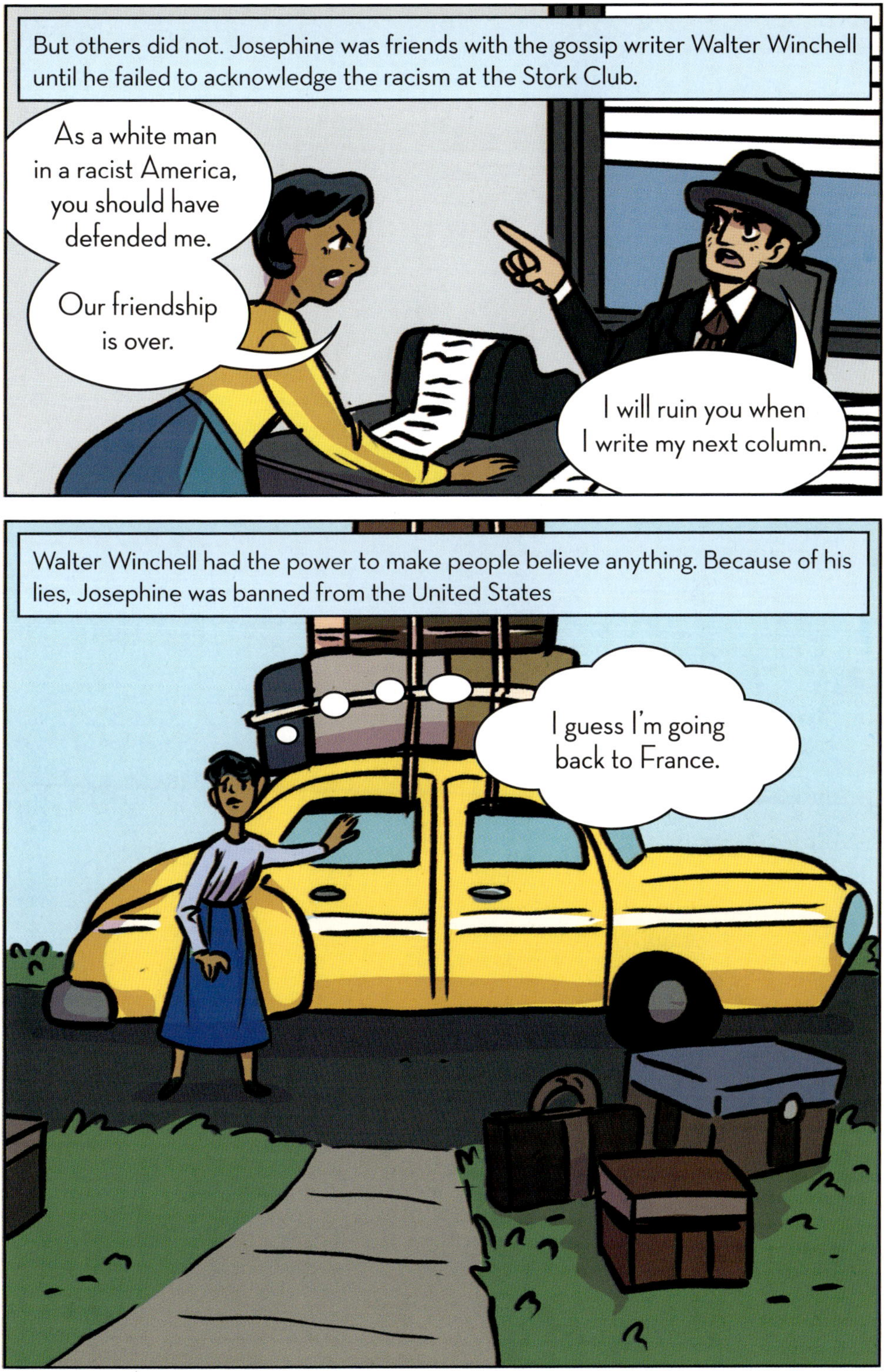
But others did not. Josephine was friends with the gossip writer Walter Winchell until he failed to acknowledge the racism at the Stork Club.
As a white man in a racist America, you should have defended me.
Our friendship is over.
I will ruin you when I write my next column.
Walter Winchell had the power to make people believe anything. Because of his lies, Josephine was banned from the United States
I guess I'm going back to France.

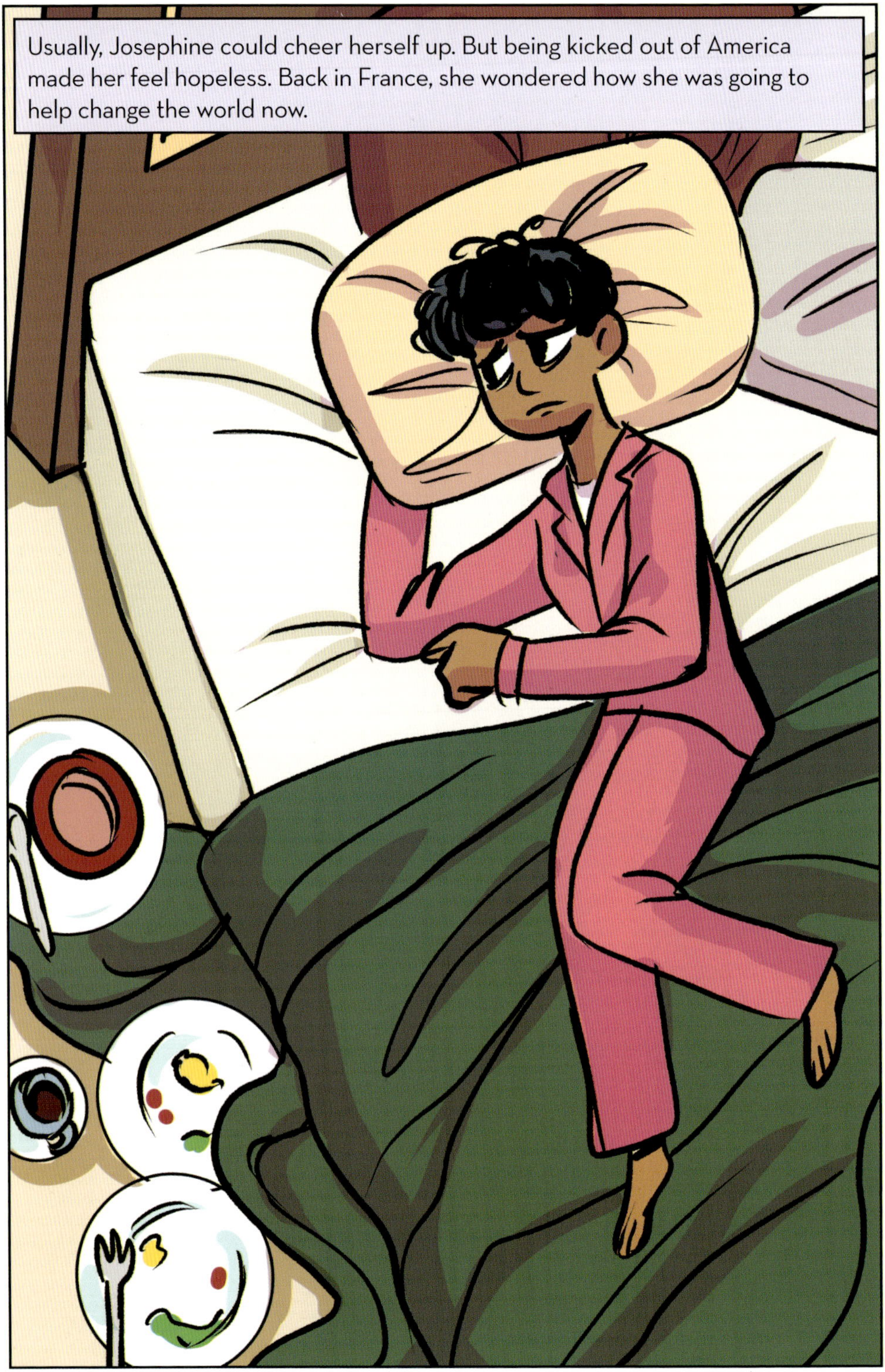
Usually, Josephine could cheer herself up. But being kicked out of America made her feel hopeless. Back in France, she wondered how she was going to help change the world now.

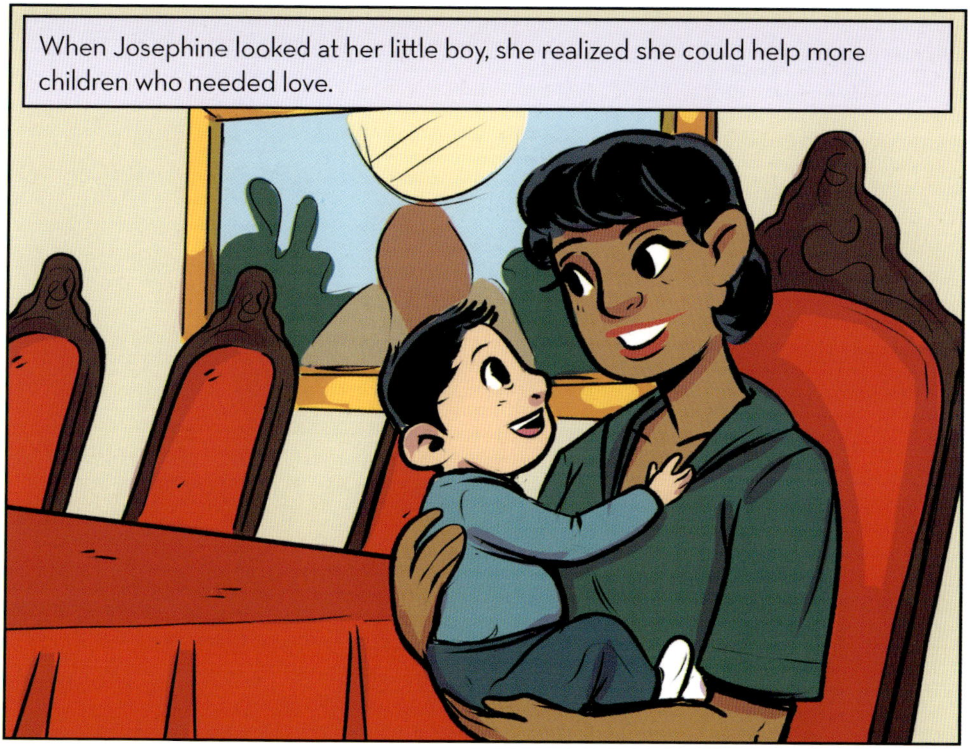
When Josephine looked at her little boy, she realized she could help more children who needed love.

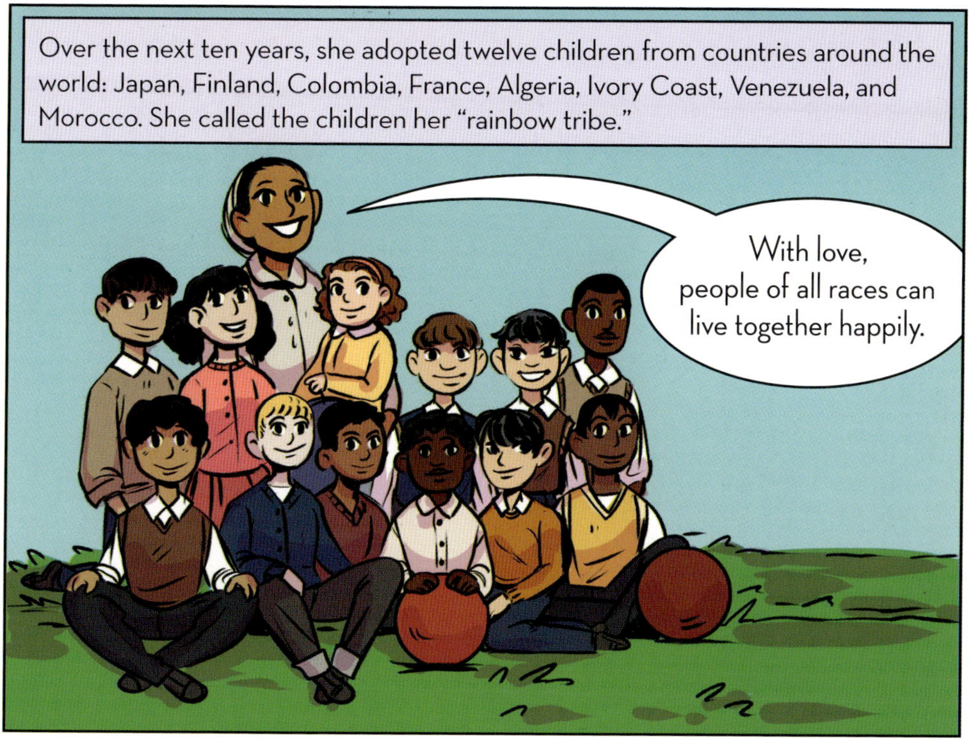
Over the next ten years, she adopted twelve children from countries around the world: Japan, Finland, Colombia, France, Algeria, Ivory Coast, Venezuela, and Morocco. She called the children her "rainbow tribe."
With love, people of all races can live together happily.

Josephine threw parties almost every weekend to show people how happy life could be if we all accepted each other.

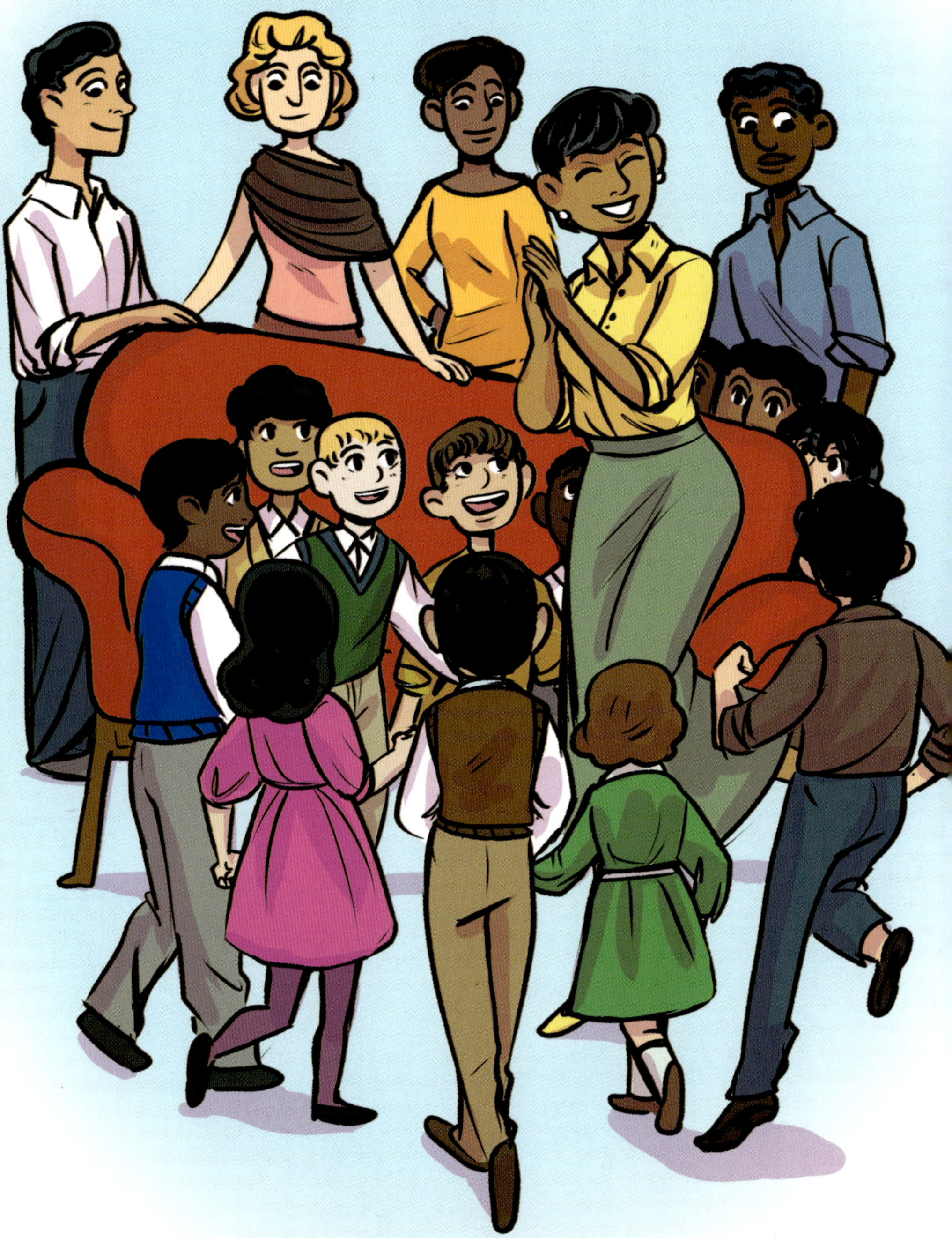

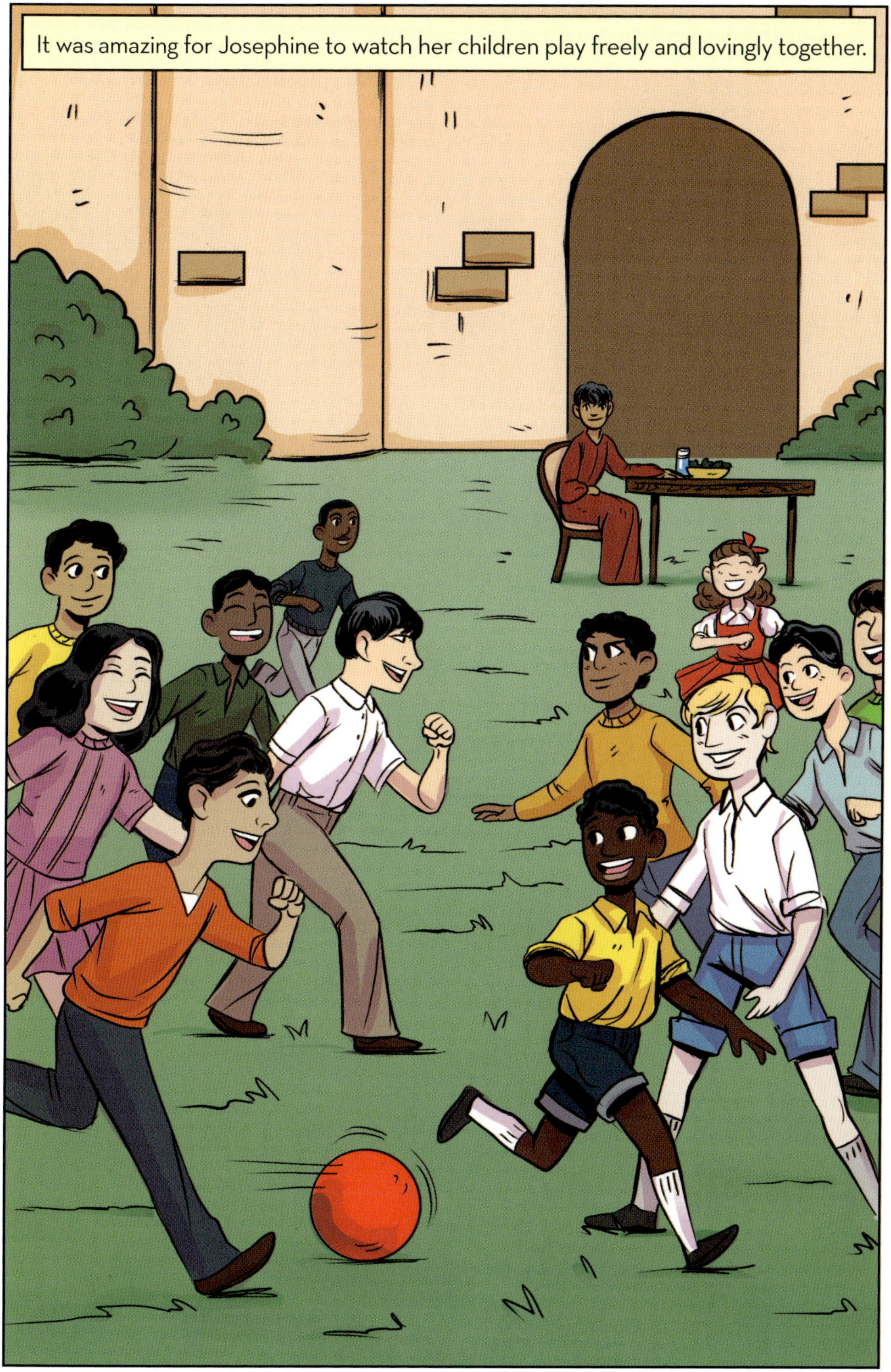
It was amazing for Josephine to watch her children play freely and lovingly together.

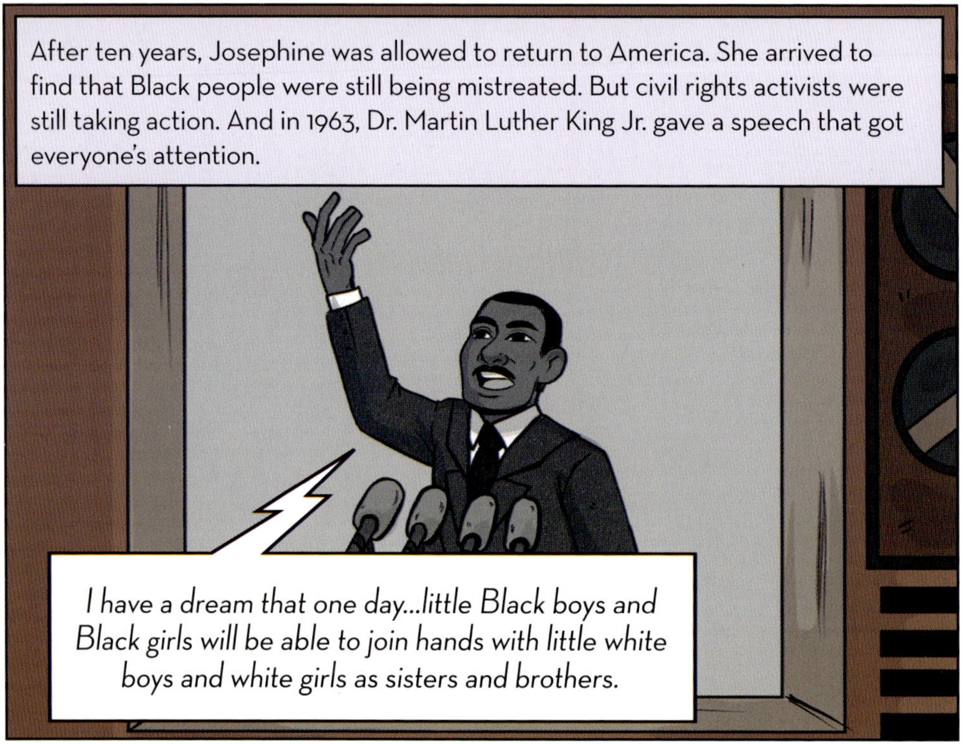
After ten years, Josephine was allowed to return to America. She arrived to find that Black people were still being mistreated. But civil rights activists were still taking action. And in 1963, Dr. Martin Luther King Jr. gave a speech that got everyone's attention.
I have a dream that one day...little Black boys and Black girls will be able to join hands with little white boys and white girls as sisters and brothers.

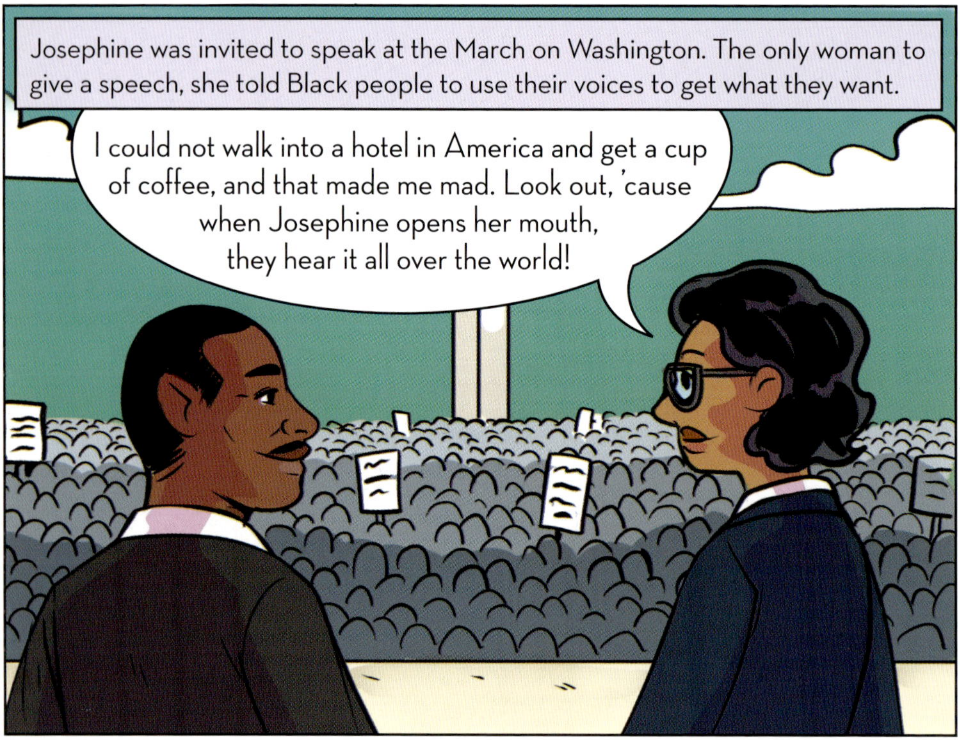
Josephine was invited to speak at the March on Washington. The only woman to give a speech, she told Black people to use their voices to get what they want.
I could not walk into a hotel in America and get a cup of coffee, and that made me mad. Look out, 'cause when Josephine opens her mouth, they hear it all over the world!

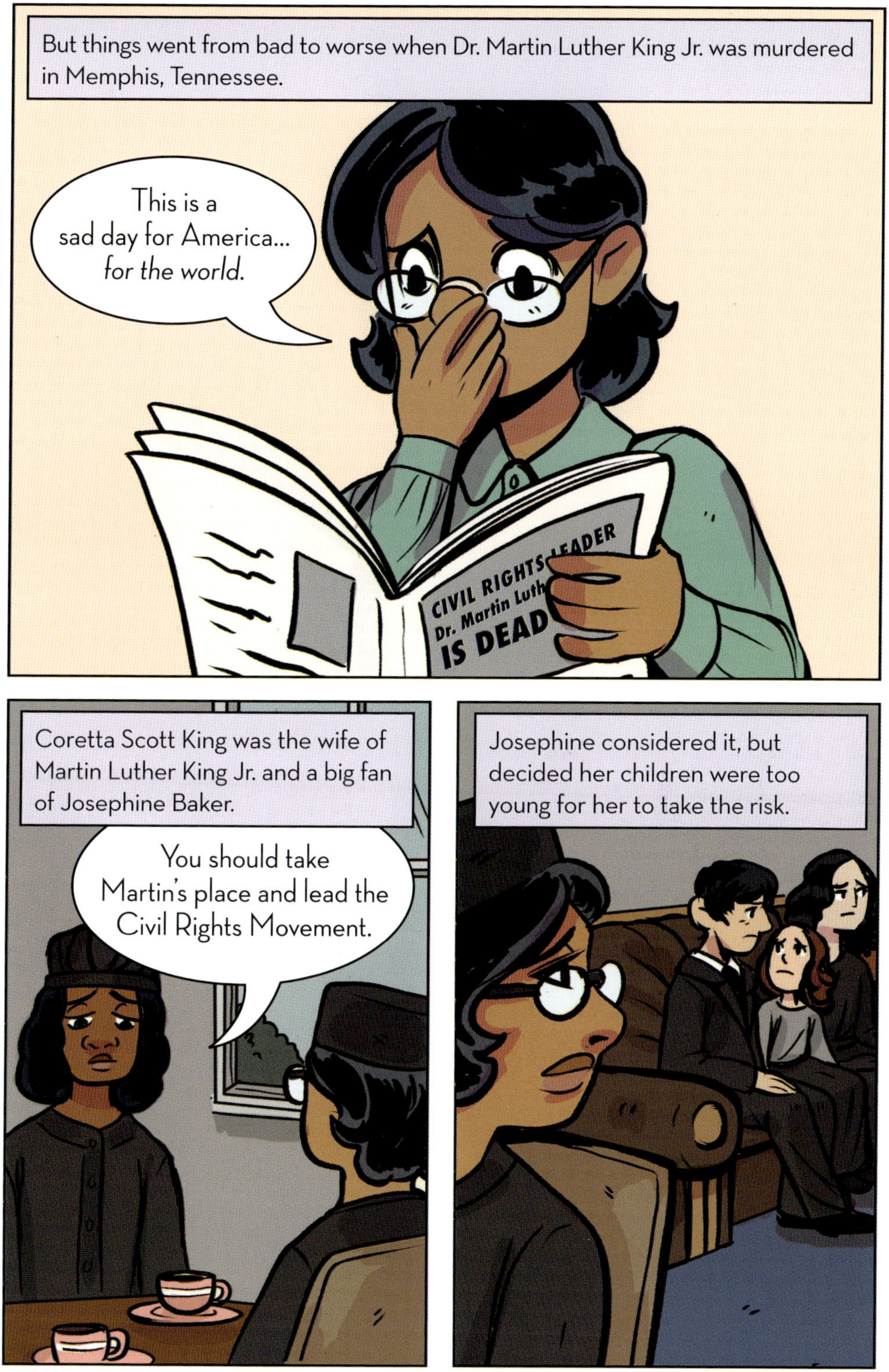

But things went from bad to worse when Dr. Martin Luther King Jr. was murdered in Memphis, Tennessee.
This is a sad day for America... *for the world.*
CIVIL RIGHTS LEADER
Dr. Martin Luth
IS DEAD
Coretta Scott King was the wife of Martin Luther King Jr. and a big fan of Josephine Baker.
You should take Martin's place and lead the Civil Rights Movement.
Josephine considered it, but decided her children were too young for her to take the risk.

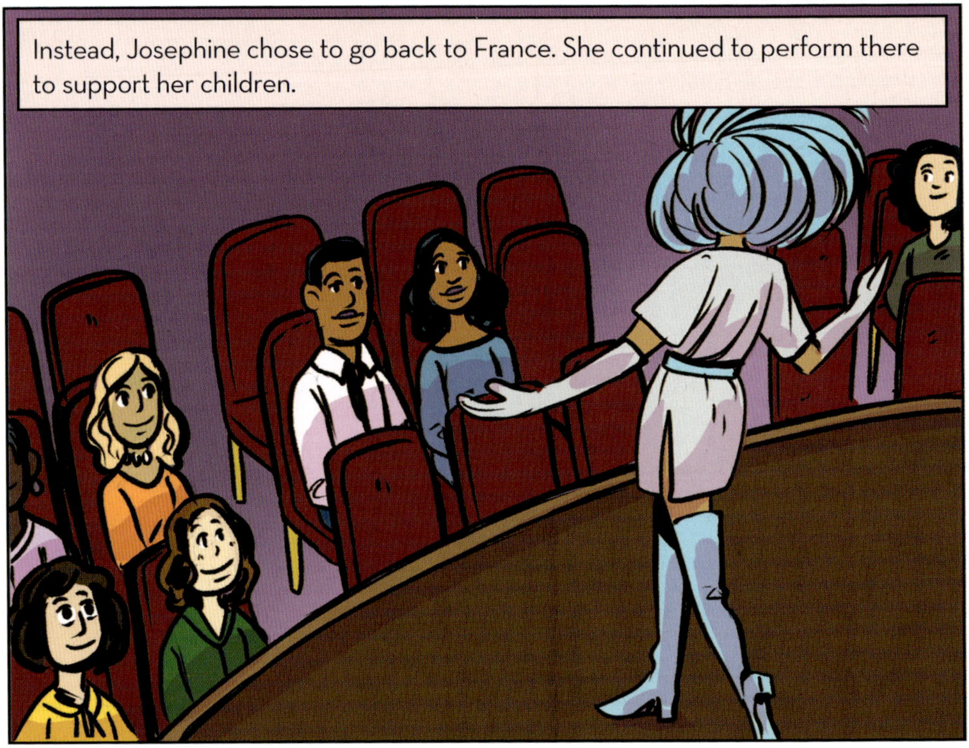
Instead, Josephine chose to go back to France. She continued to perform there to support her children.

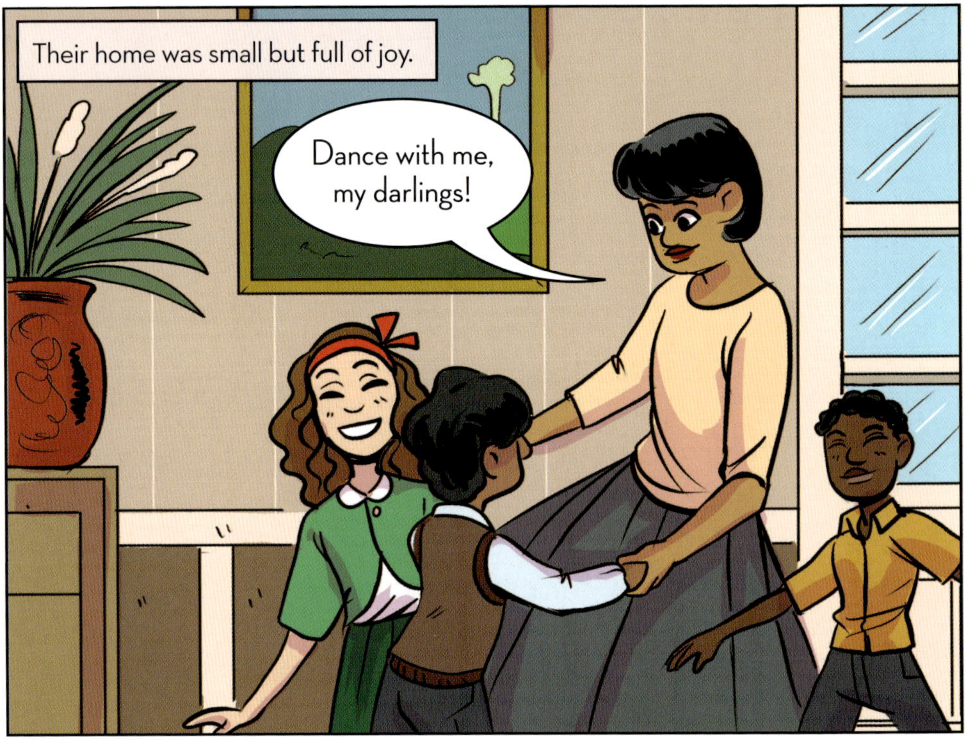
Their home was small but full of joy.
Dance with me, my darlings!

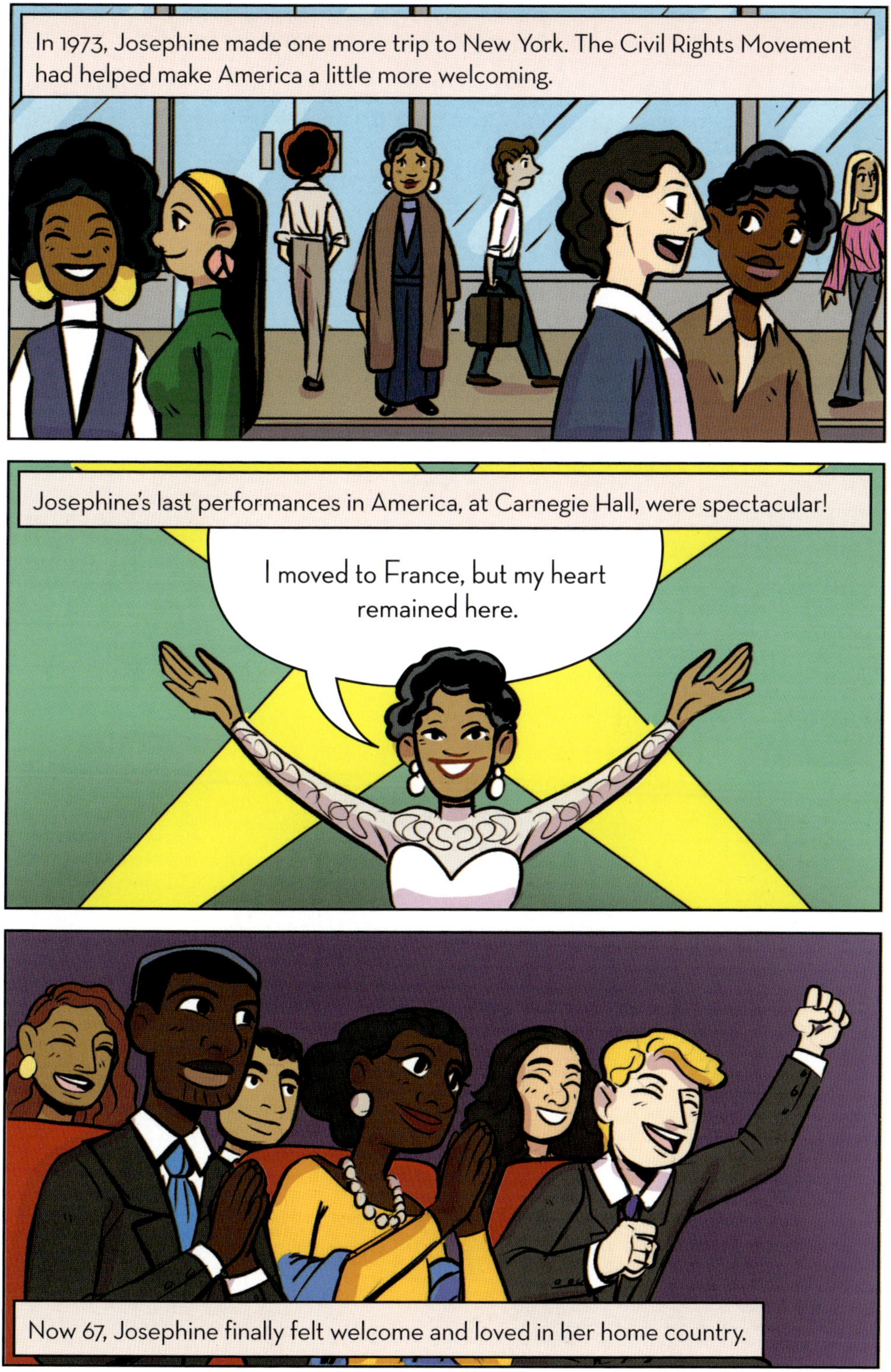
In 1973, Josephine made one more trip to New York. The Civil Rights Movement had helped make America a little more welcoming.
Josephine's last performances in America, at Carnegie Hall, were spectacular!
I moved to France, but my heart remained here.
Now 67, Josephine finally felt welcome and loved in her home country.

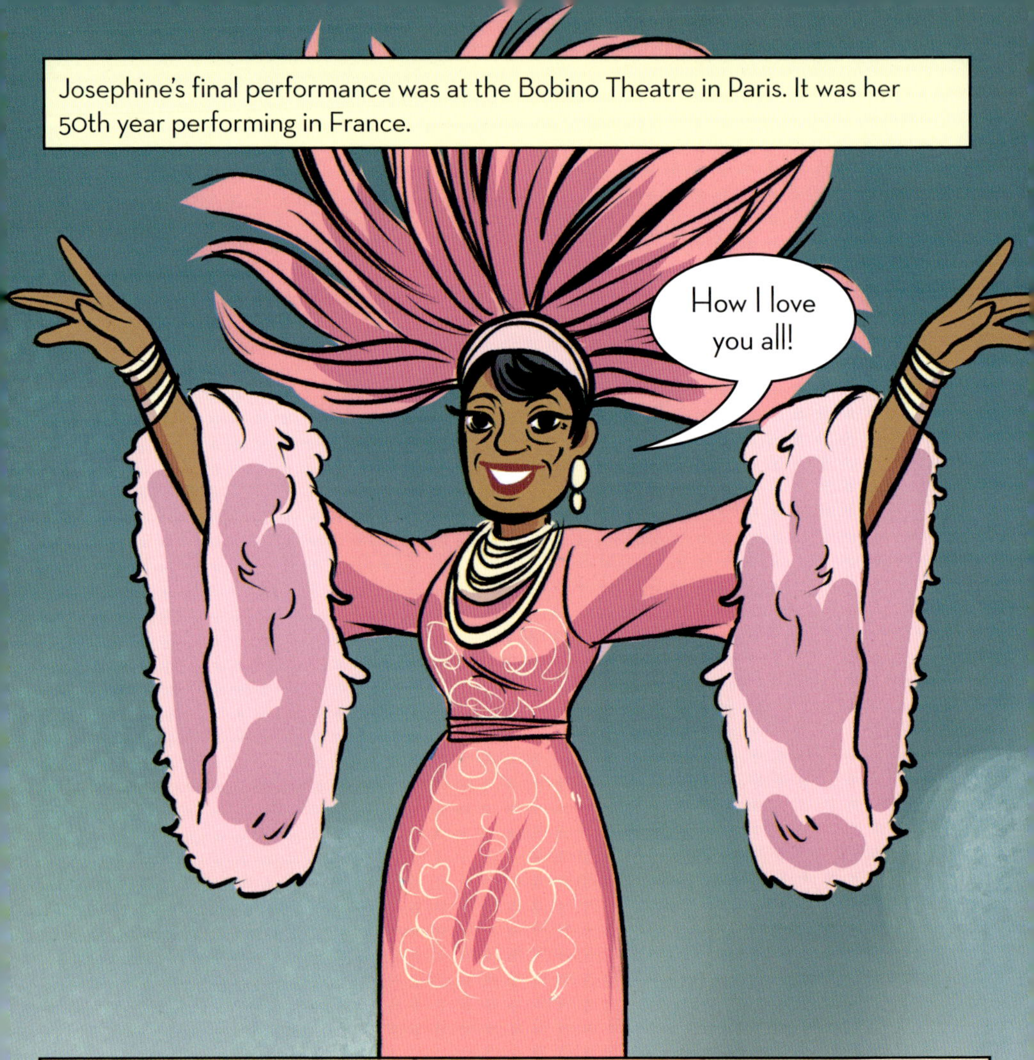
Josephine's final performance was at the Bobino Theatre in Paris. It was her 50th year performing in France.
How I love you all!

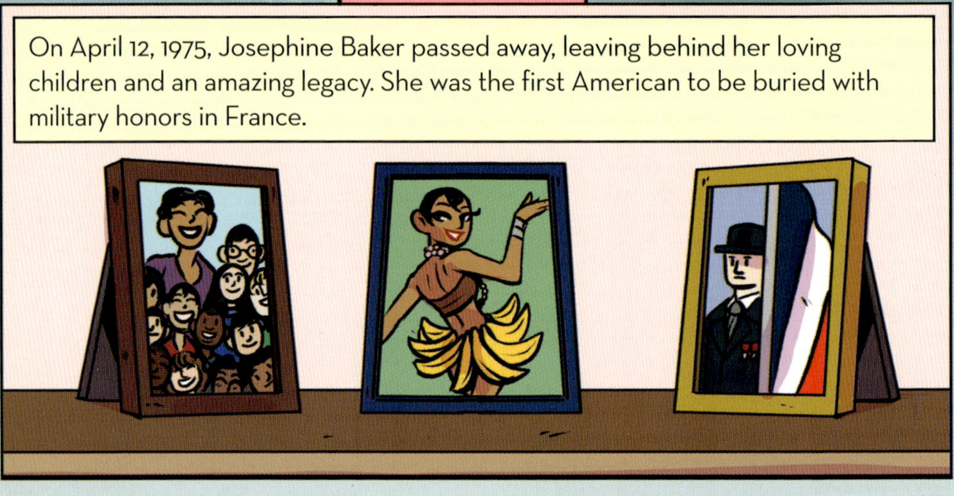
On April 12, 1975, Josephine Baker passed away, leaving behind her loving children and an amazing legacy. She was the first American to be buried with military honors in France.

Lauren Gamble is a multimedia writer from Mobile, Alabama. She uses her voice to tell character-driven stories about Black female artists through television, novels, and audio stories. This book is dedicated to her nieces Zoë and Milan, two little Black girls who now have the opportunity to obtain anything their hearts desire.

Markia Jenai was raised in Detroit during rough times, and found adventure through art and storytelling. After studying at the Academy of Art in San Francisco, she made it her goal to create worlds where people of color are front and center. When she's not drawing, she likes to watch documentaries, listen to Dungeons & Dragons livestreams, and read historical articles—all of which fuels her work!

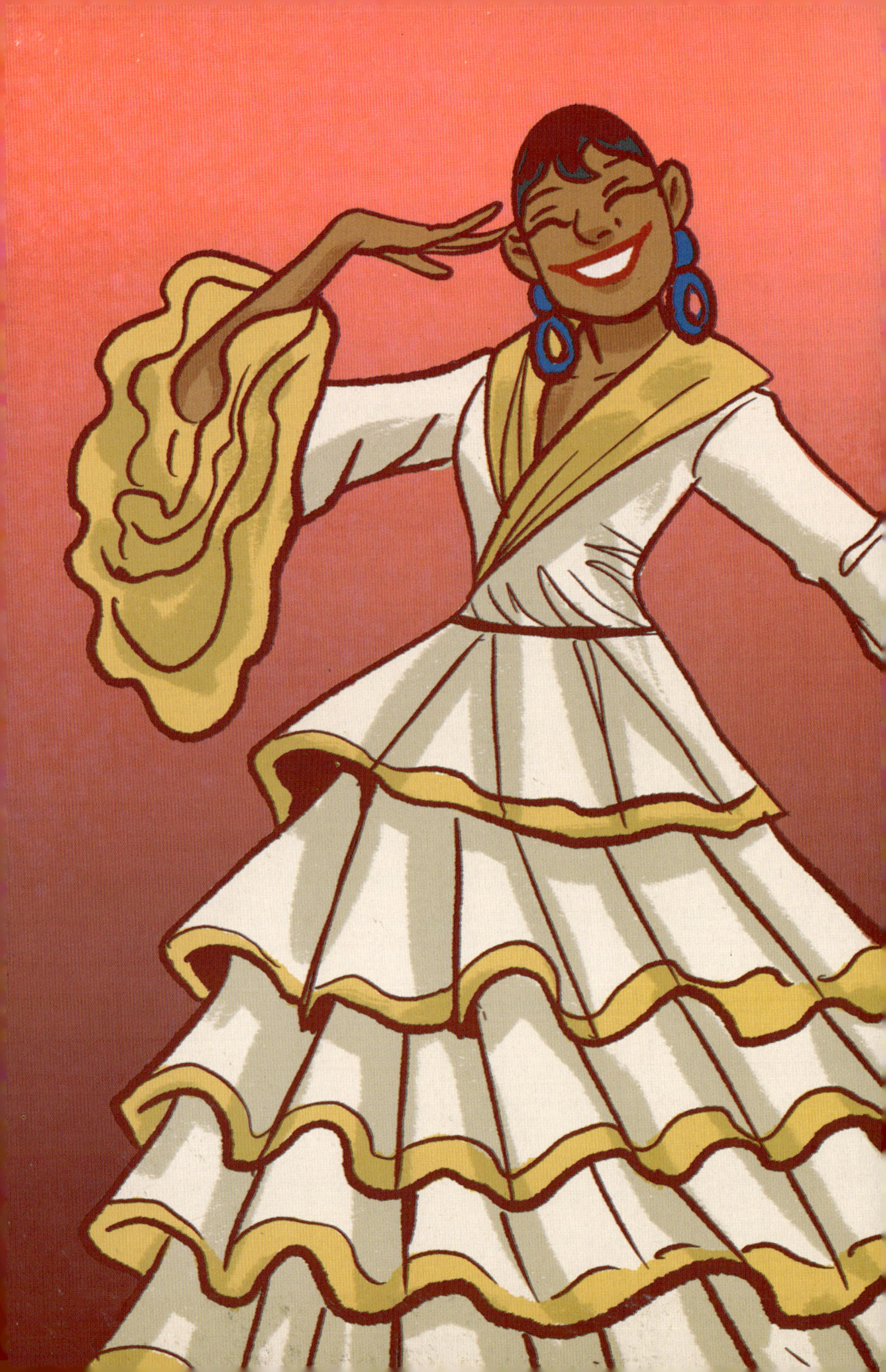